LEARN TO SPEAK CAT

FAKE MEWS

By Anthony Smith

LEARN TO SPEAK CAT FAKE MEWS

Anthony Smith

Published by Soaring Penguin Press
4 Florence Terrace
London
SW15 3RU
www.soaringpenguinpress.com

ISBN 978-1-908030-47-4

www.facebook.com/learntospeakcat
www.gocomics.com/learn-to-speak-cat

Printed in Bulgaria

Soaring Penguin Press

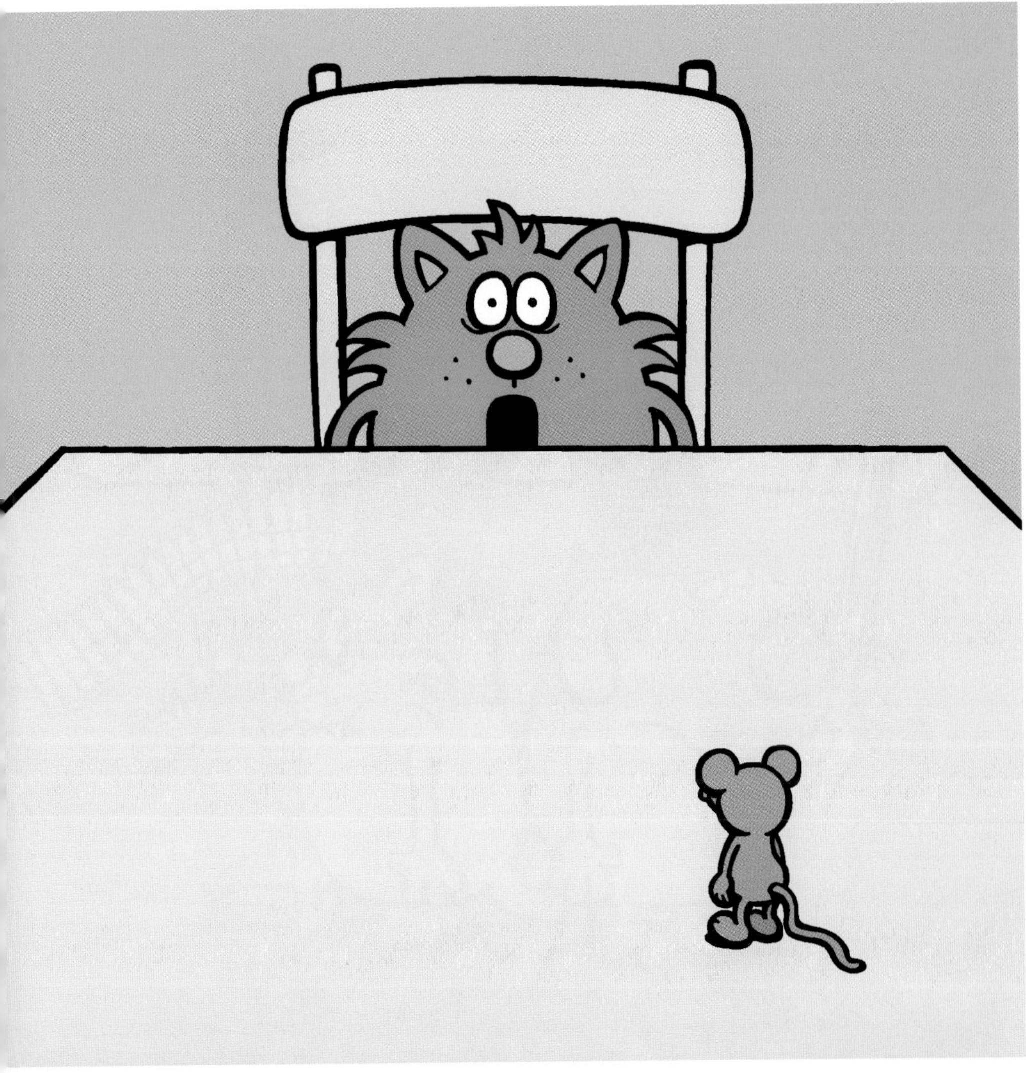

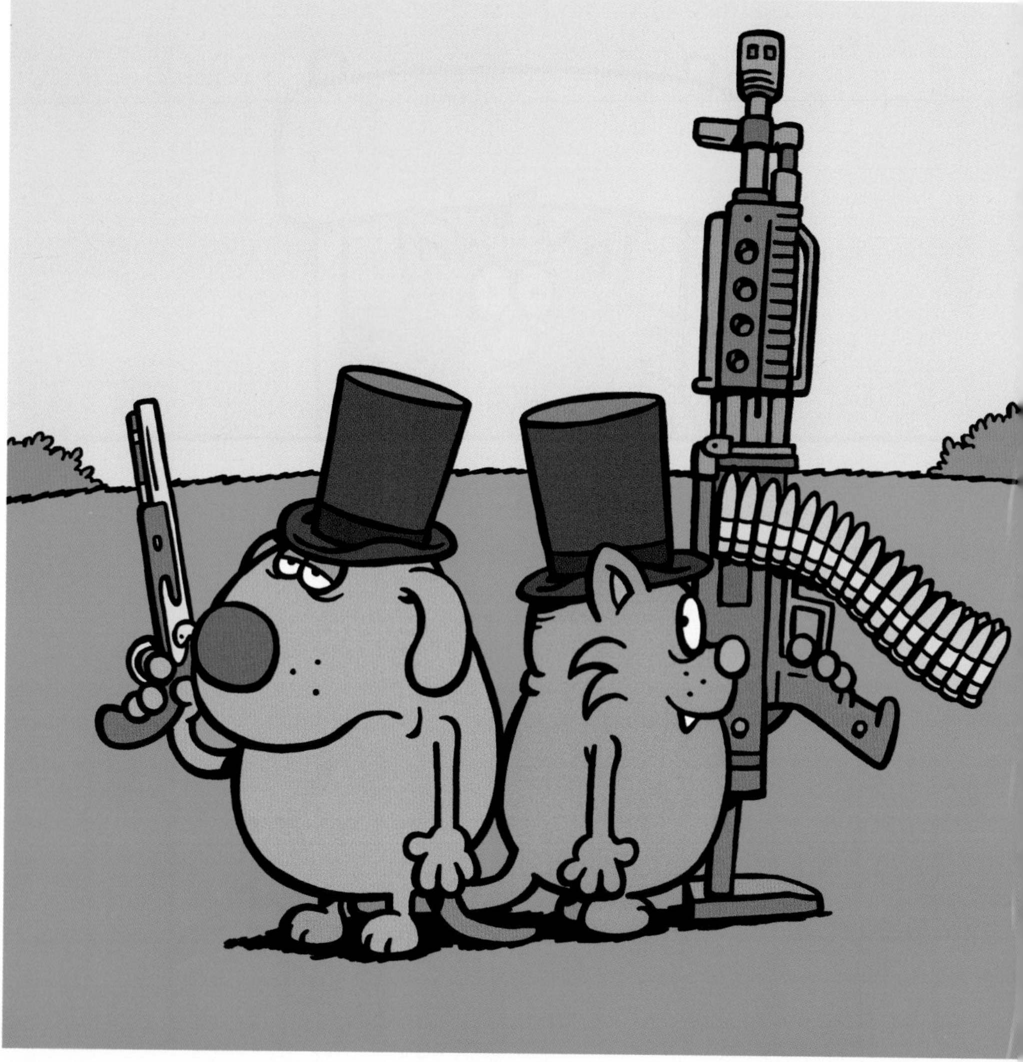

PURRSON

"Creature that operates the fridge door."

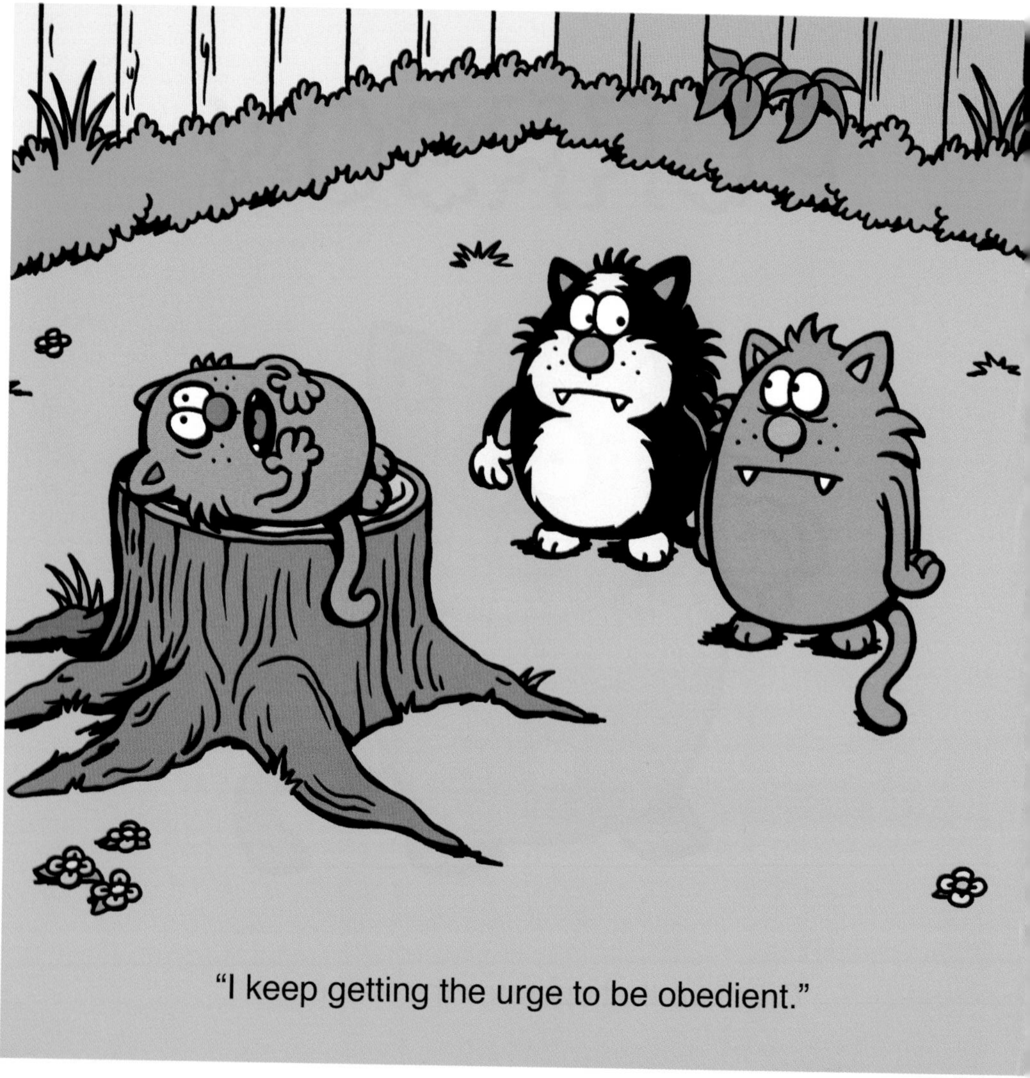

"I keep getting the urge to be obedient."

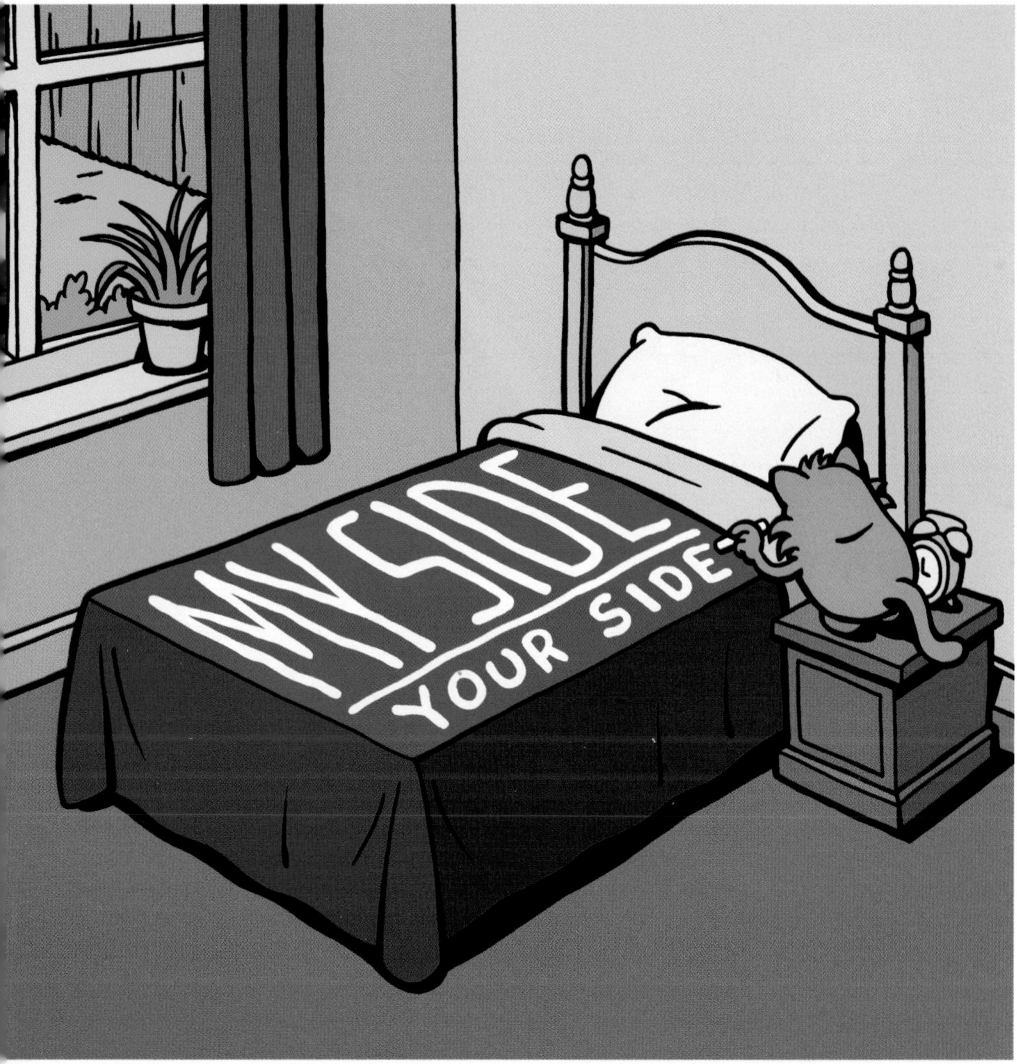
MY SIDE
YOUR SIDE

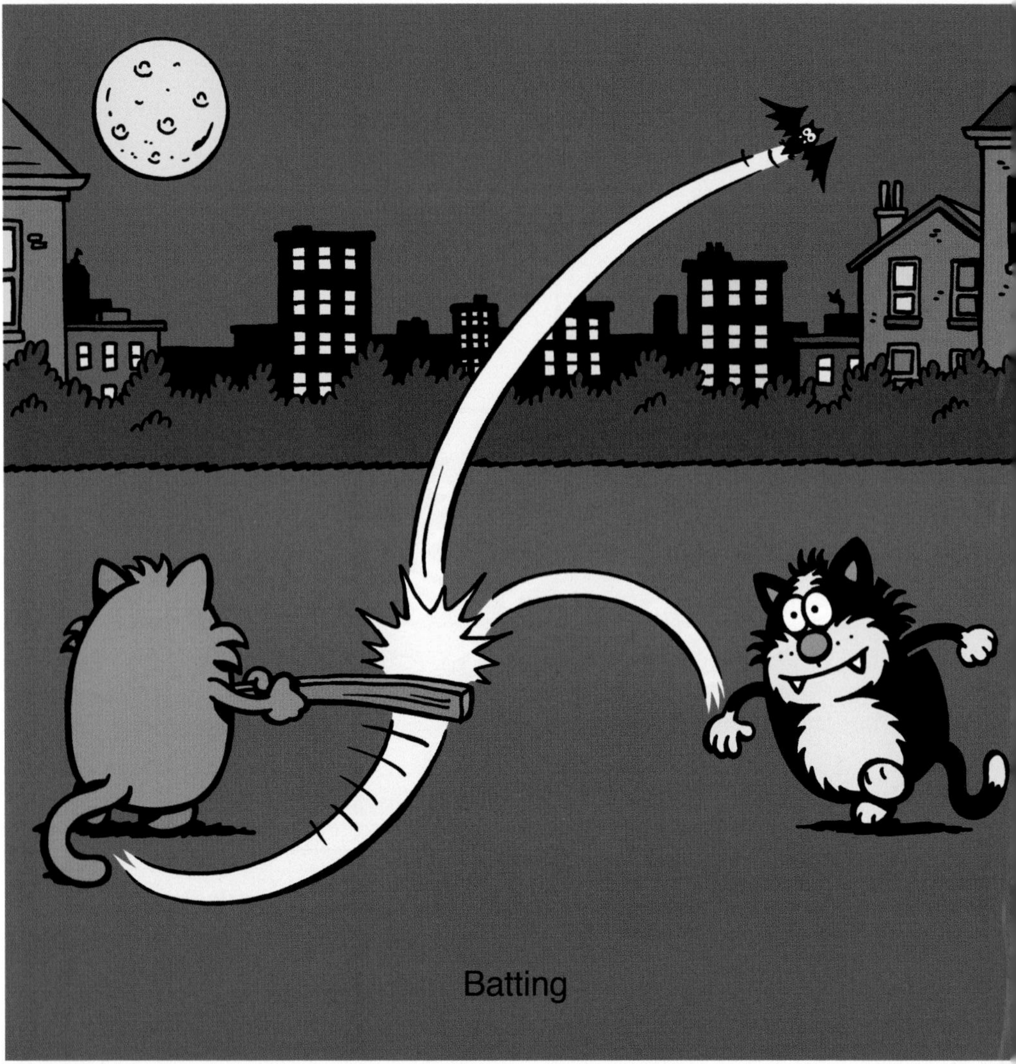

Batting

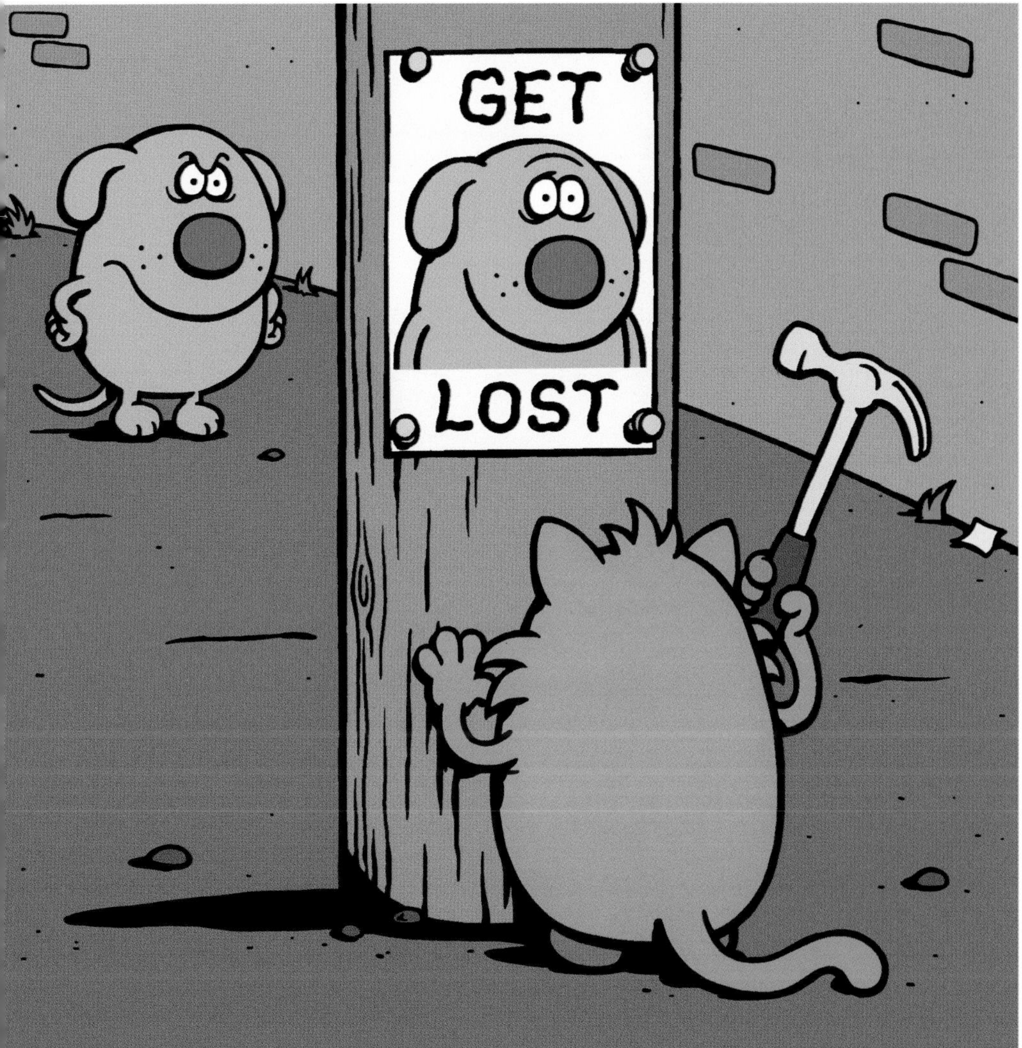
GET
LOST

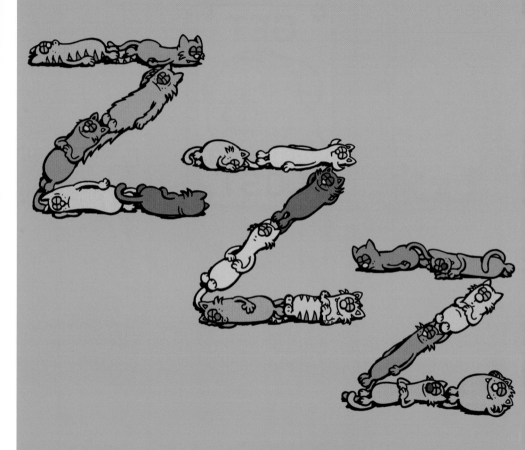

Formation napping

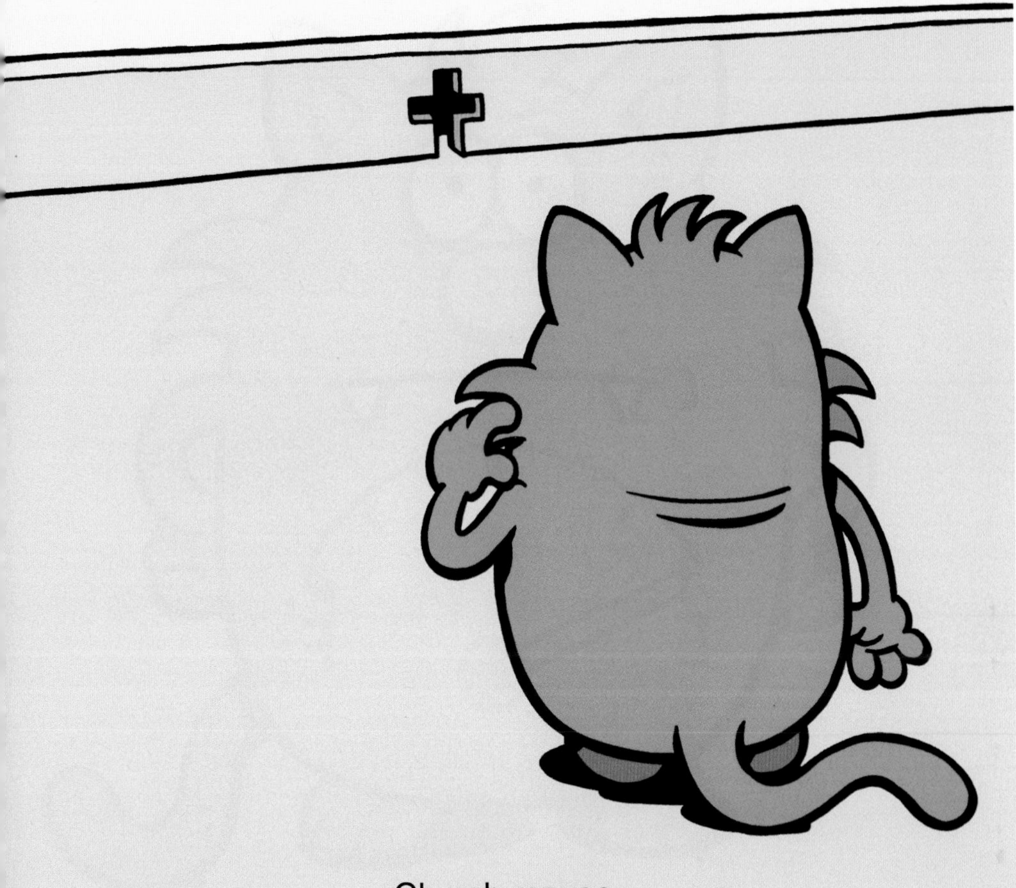

Church mouse

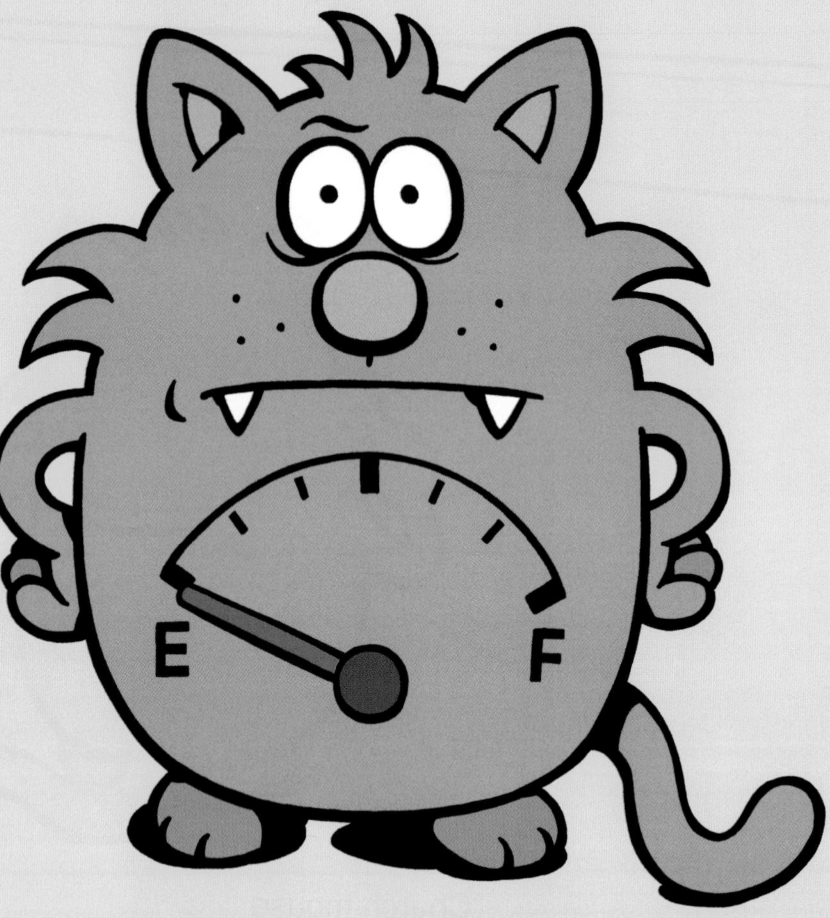
E
F

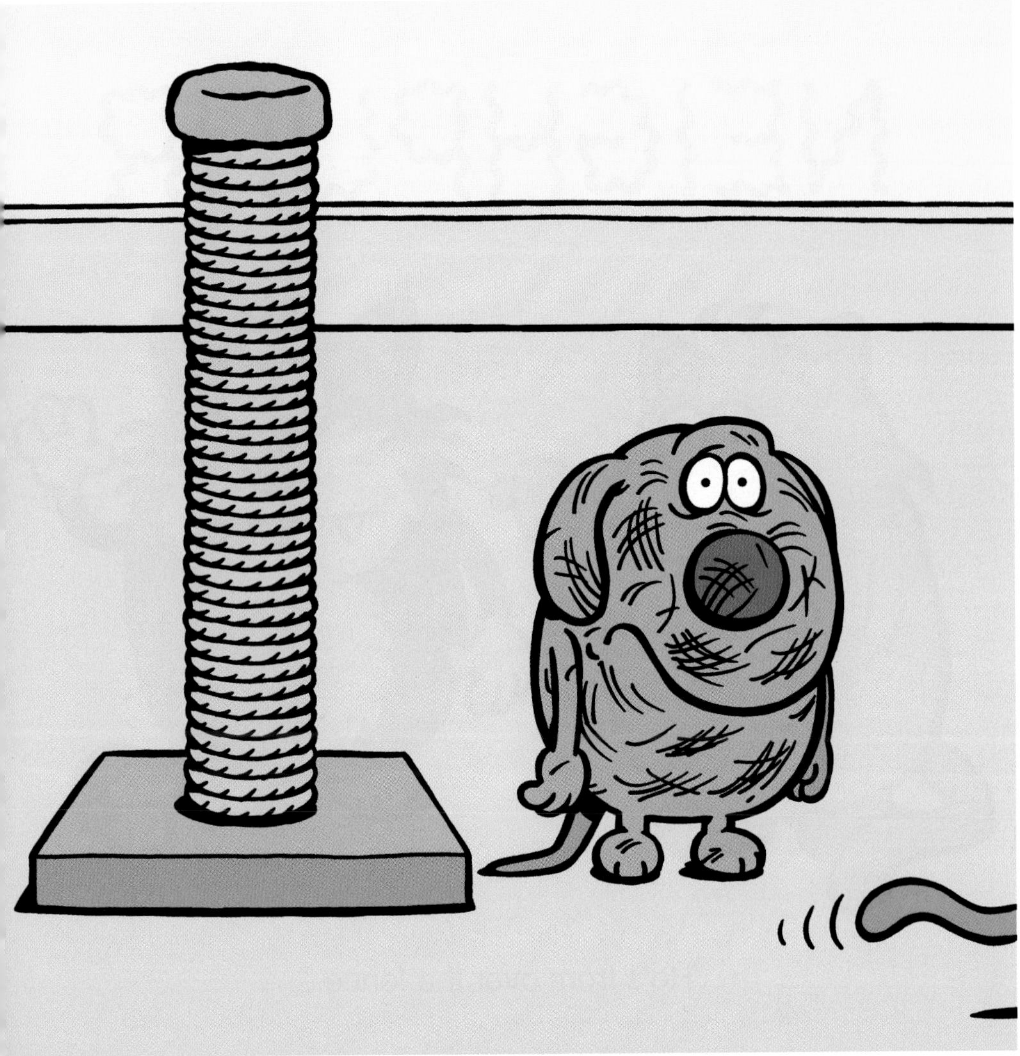

NEIGHPURR

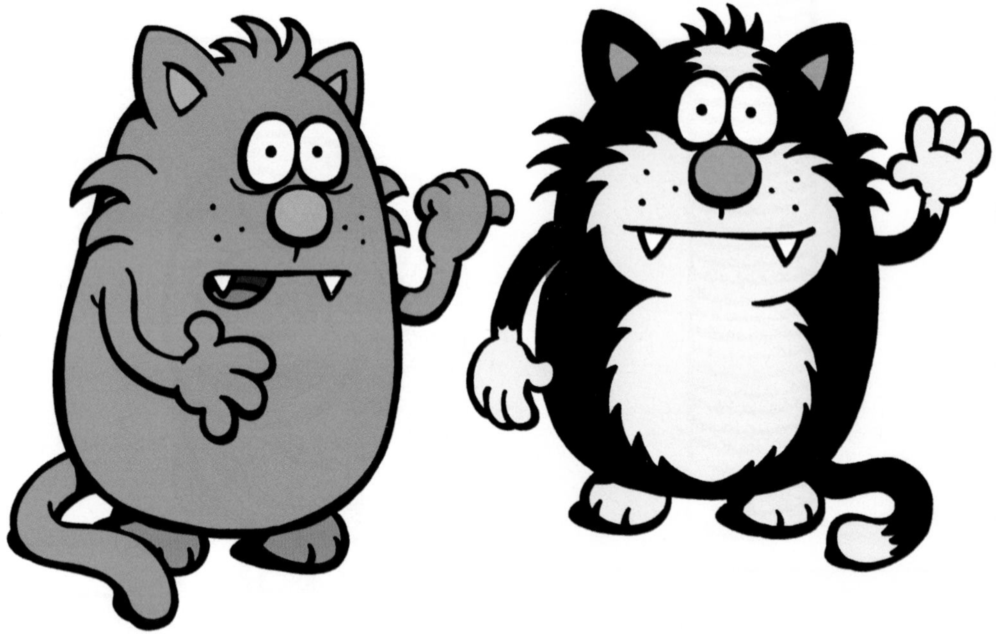

"He's from over the fence."

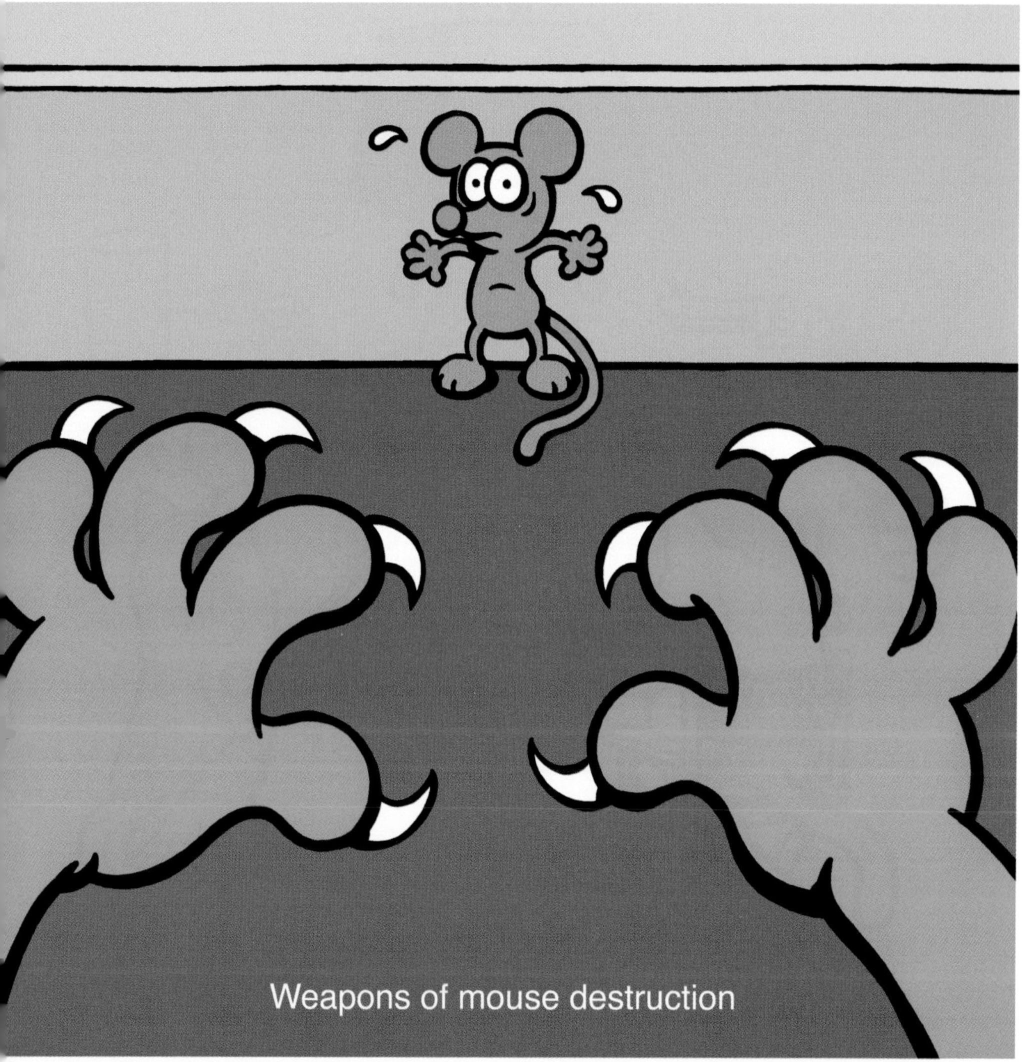

Weapons of mouse destruction

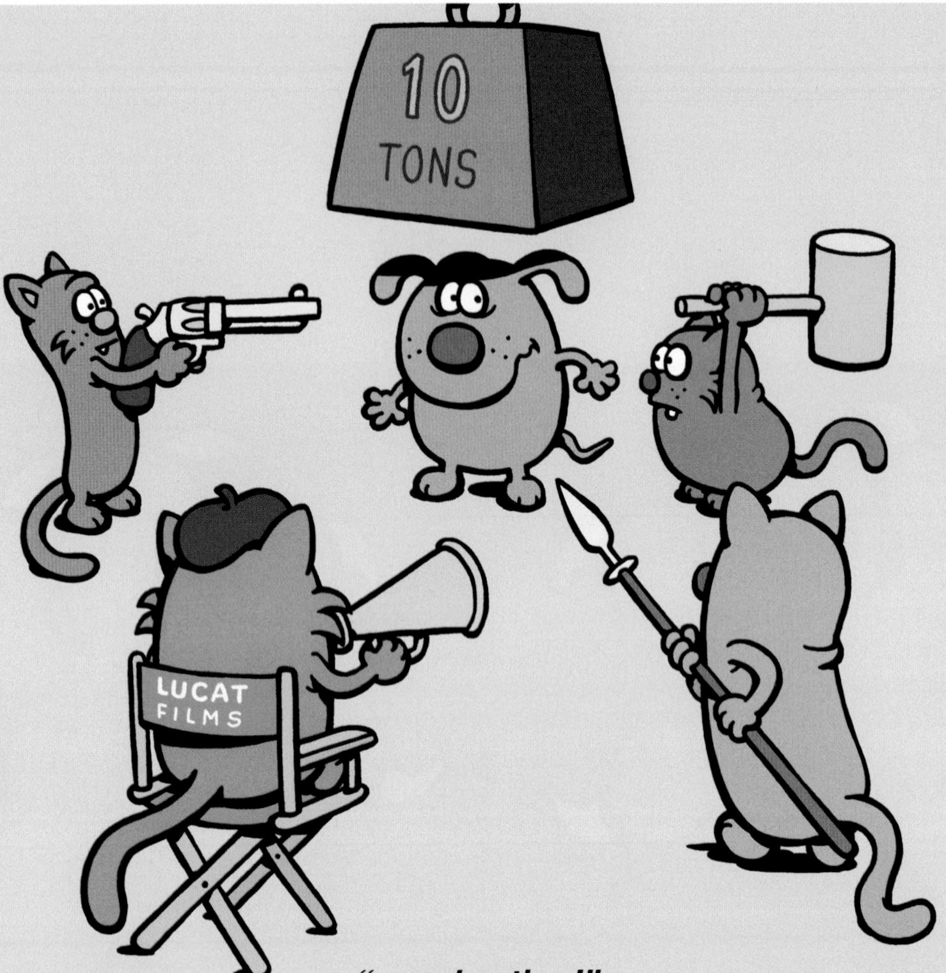
10
TONS
LUCAT
FILMS

"...and action!"

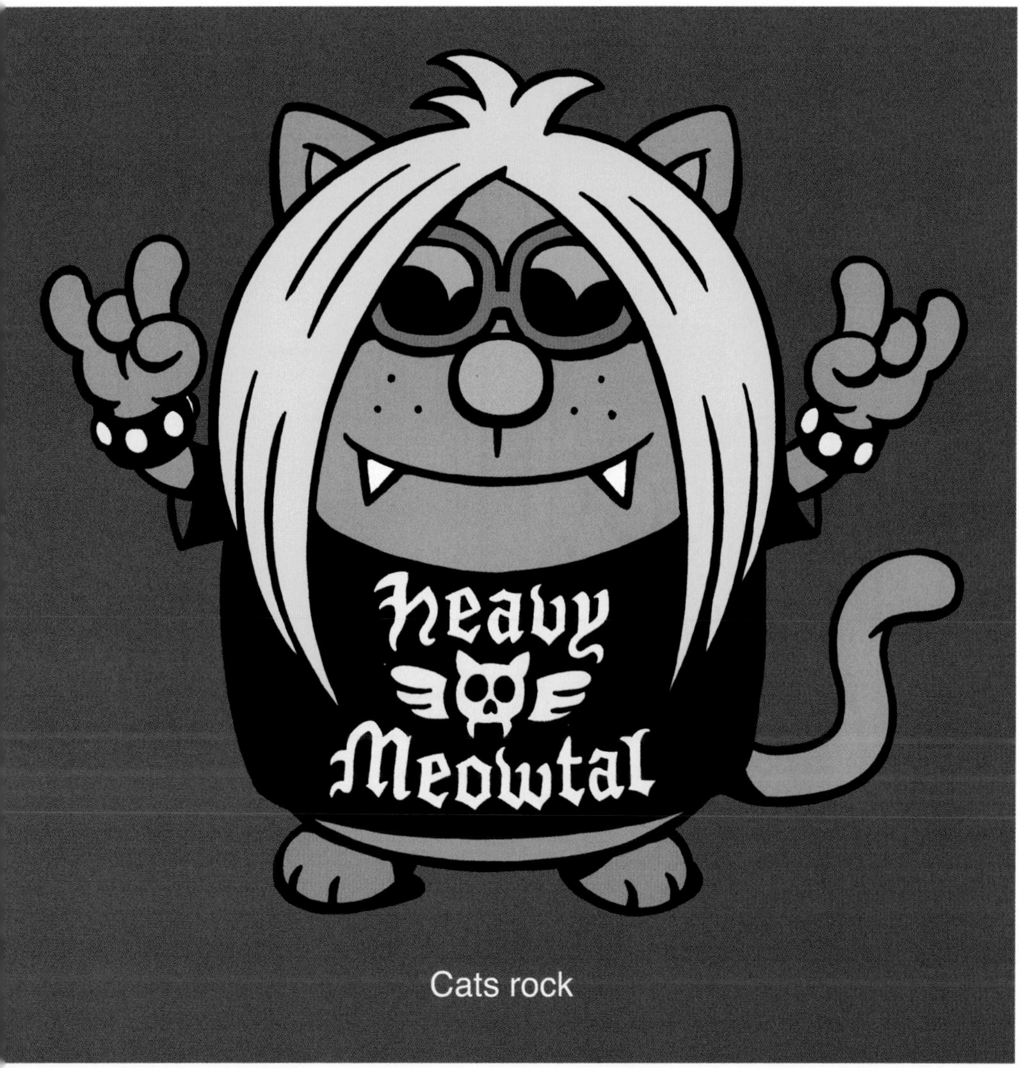
Heavy
Meowtal

Cats rock

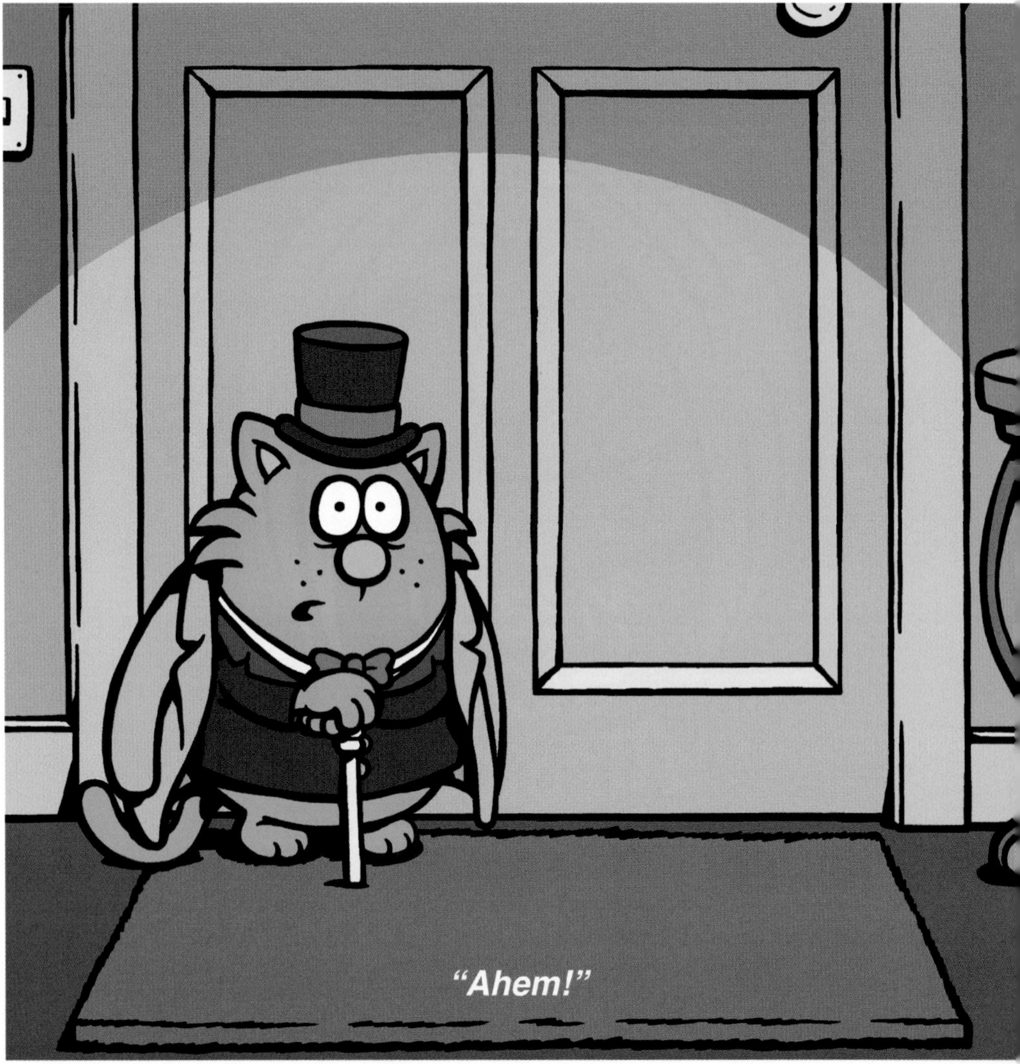
"Ahem!"

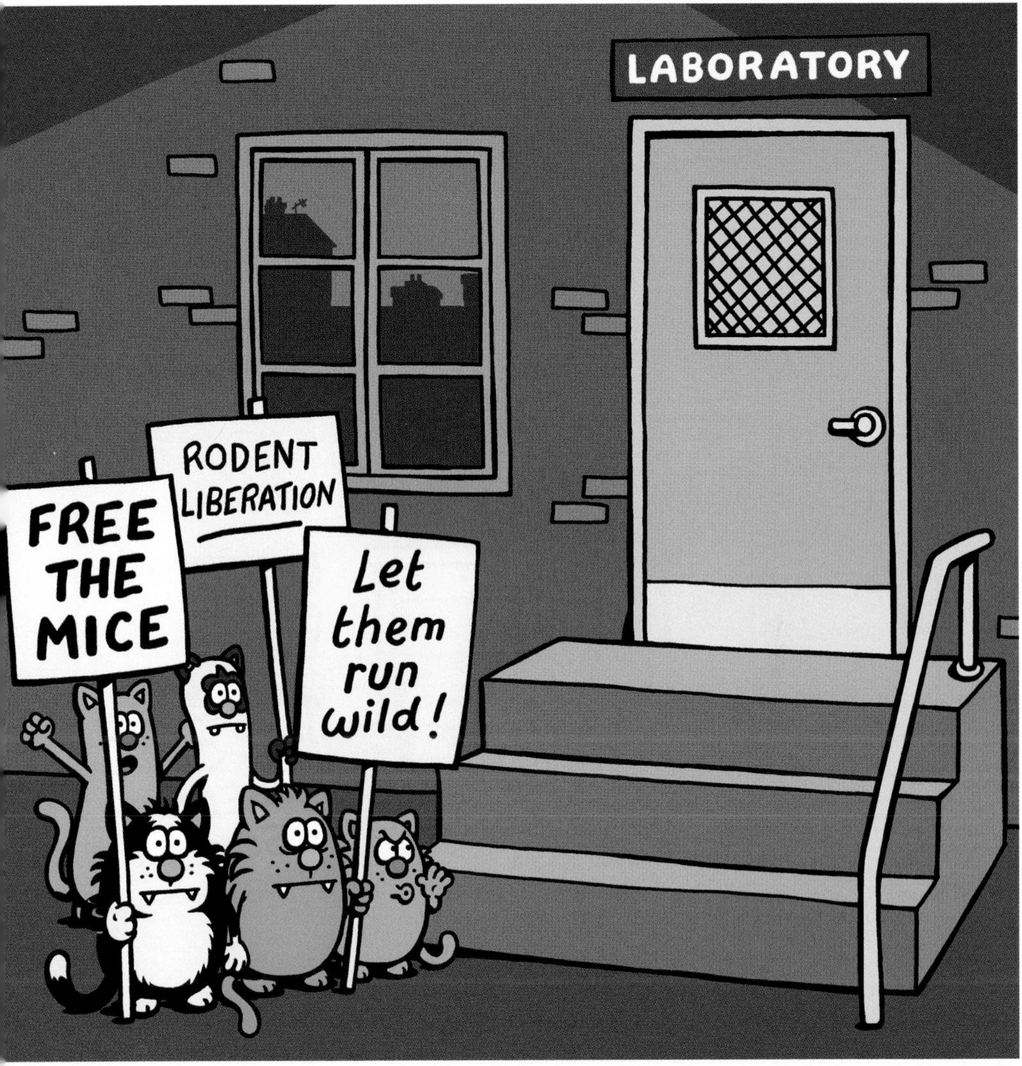
LABORATORY
RODENT LIBERATION
FREE THE MICE
Let them run wild!

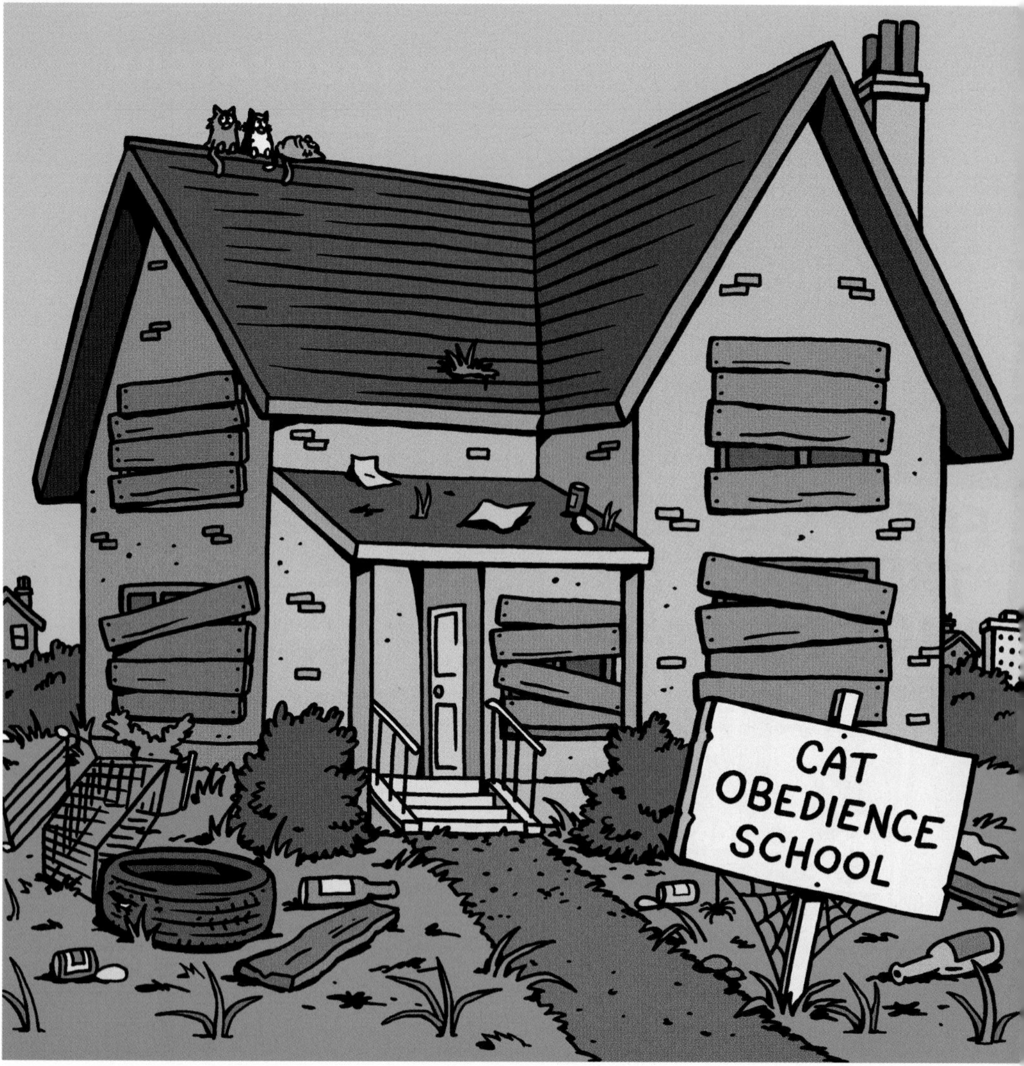
CAT
OBEDIENCE
SCHOOL

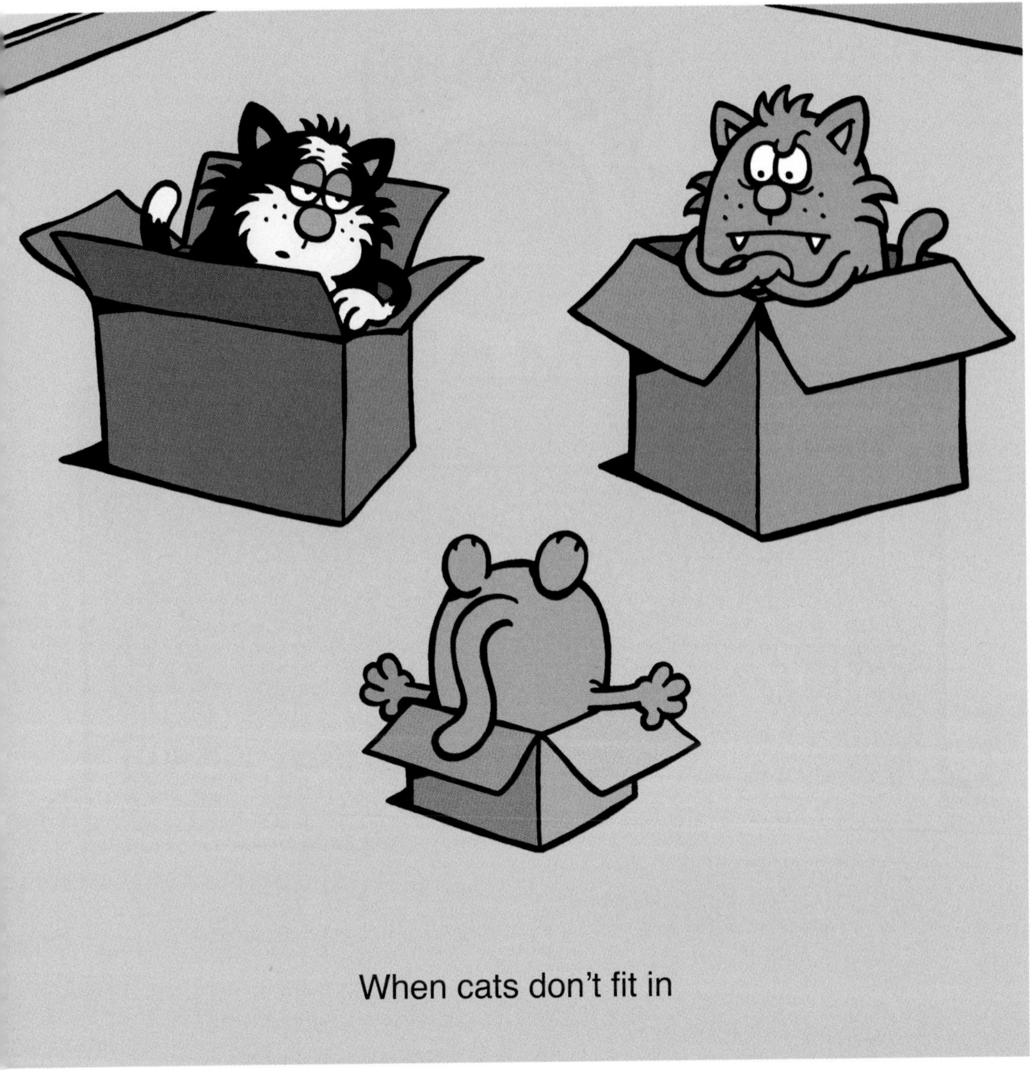

When cats don't fit in

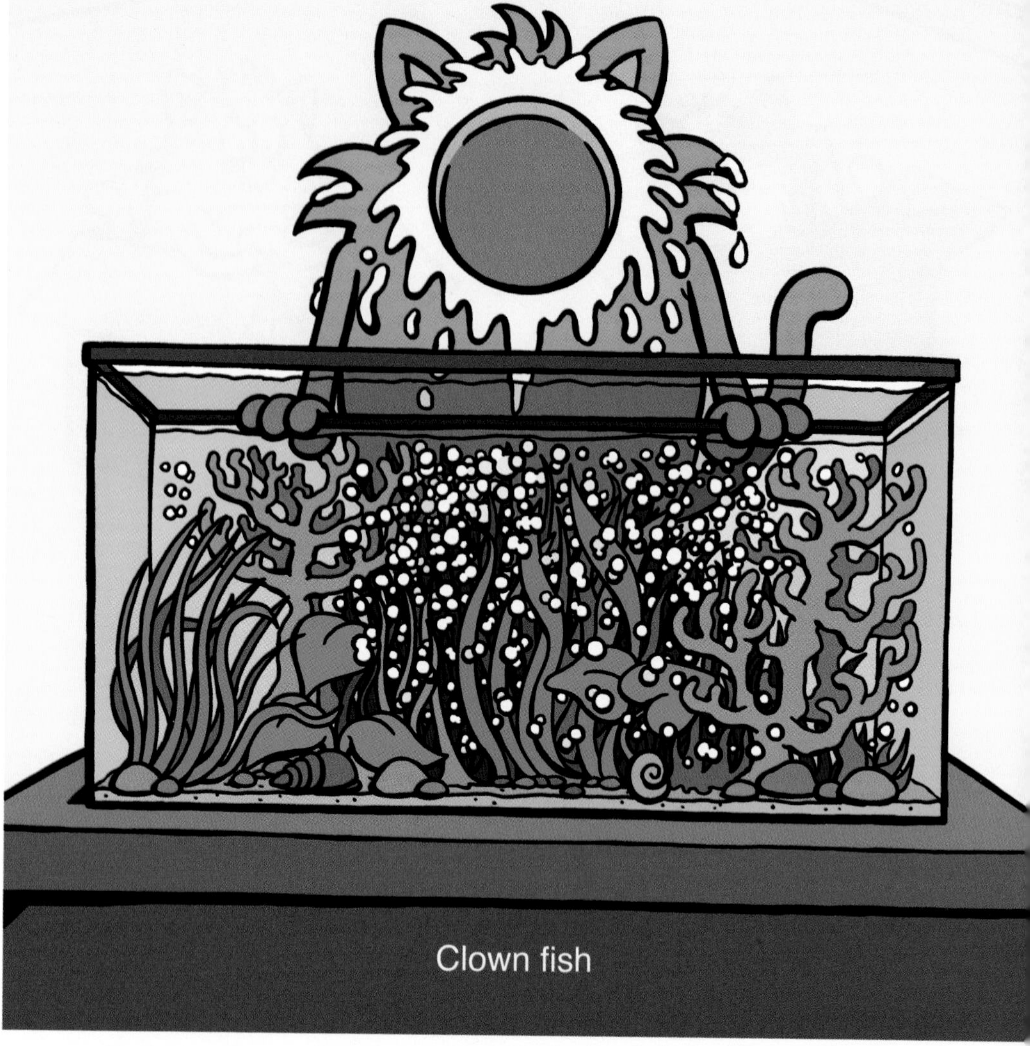

Clown fish

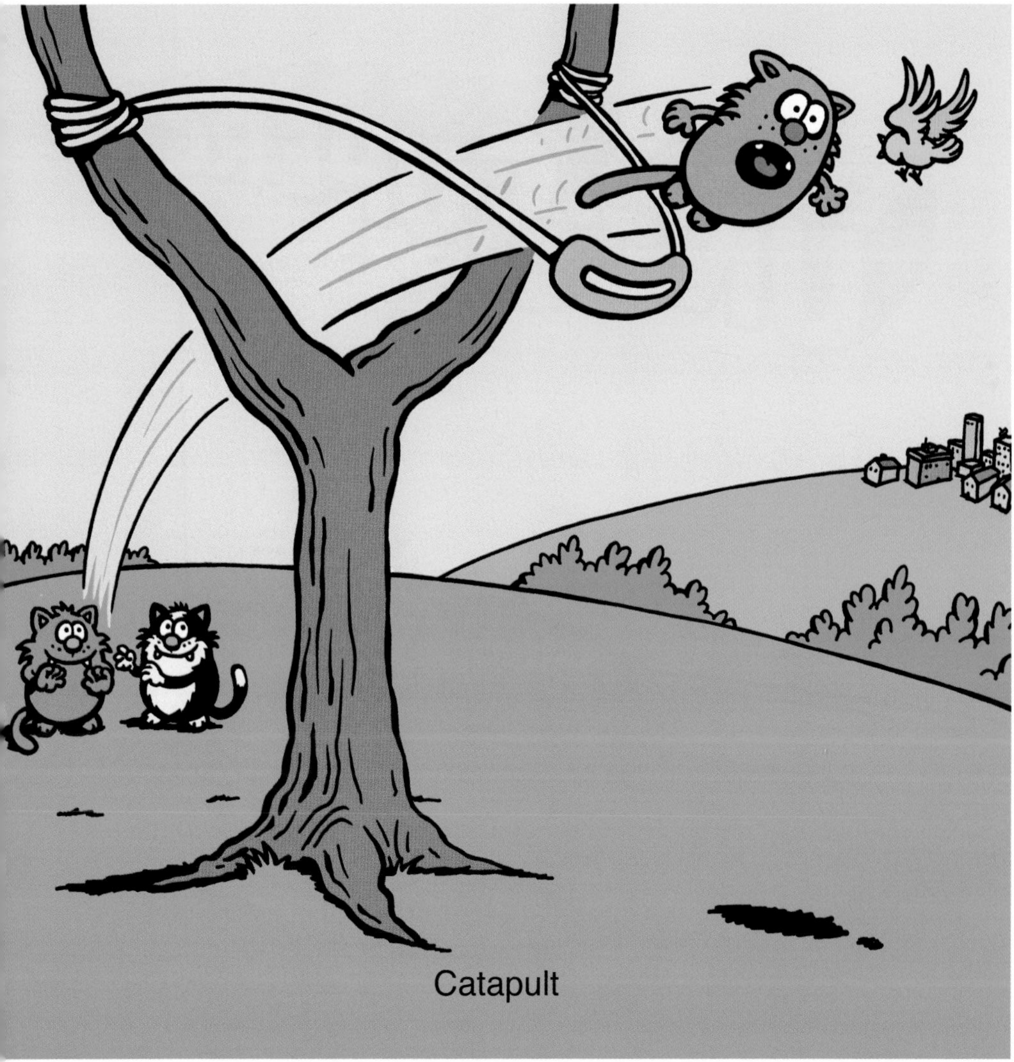

Catapult

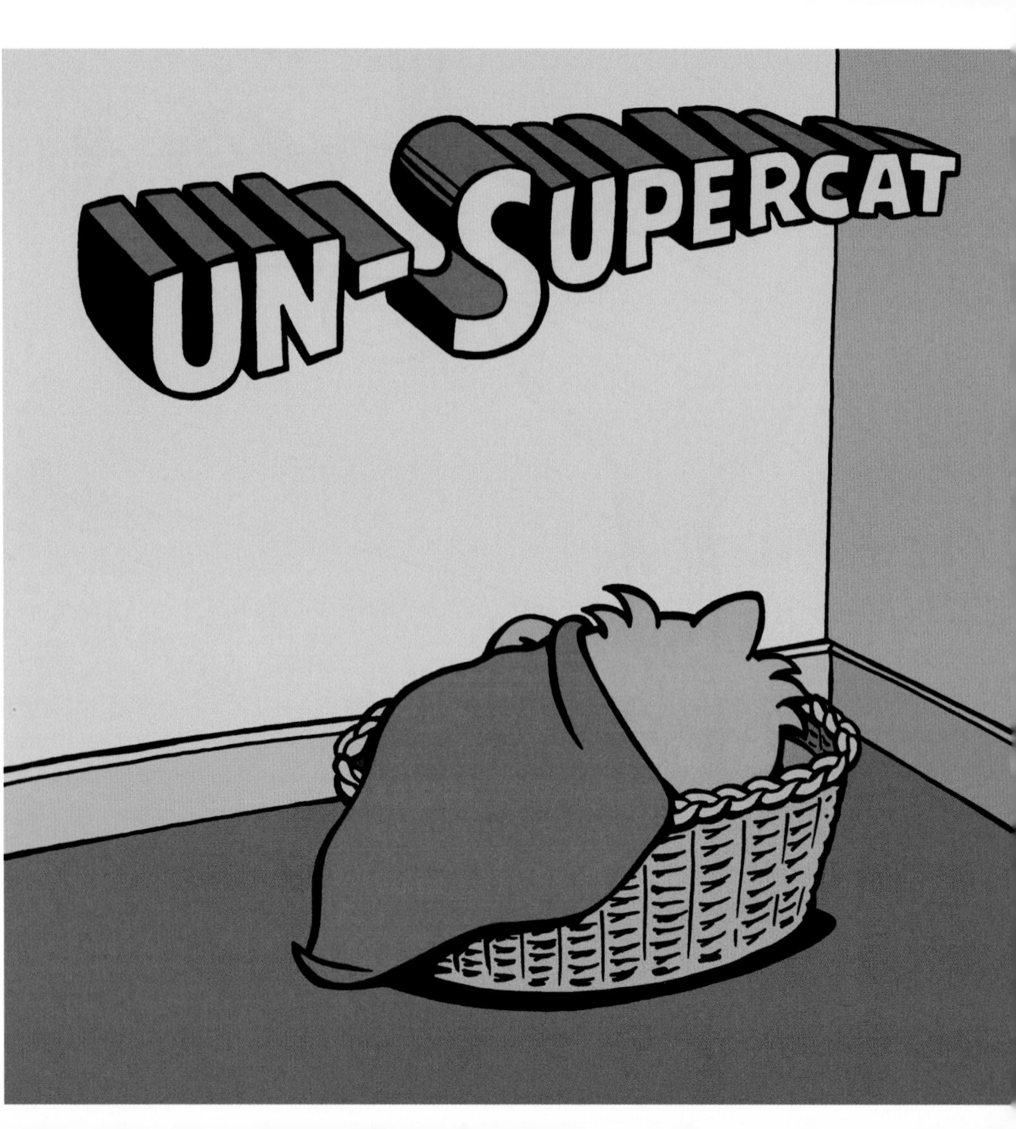
UN-SUPERCAT

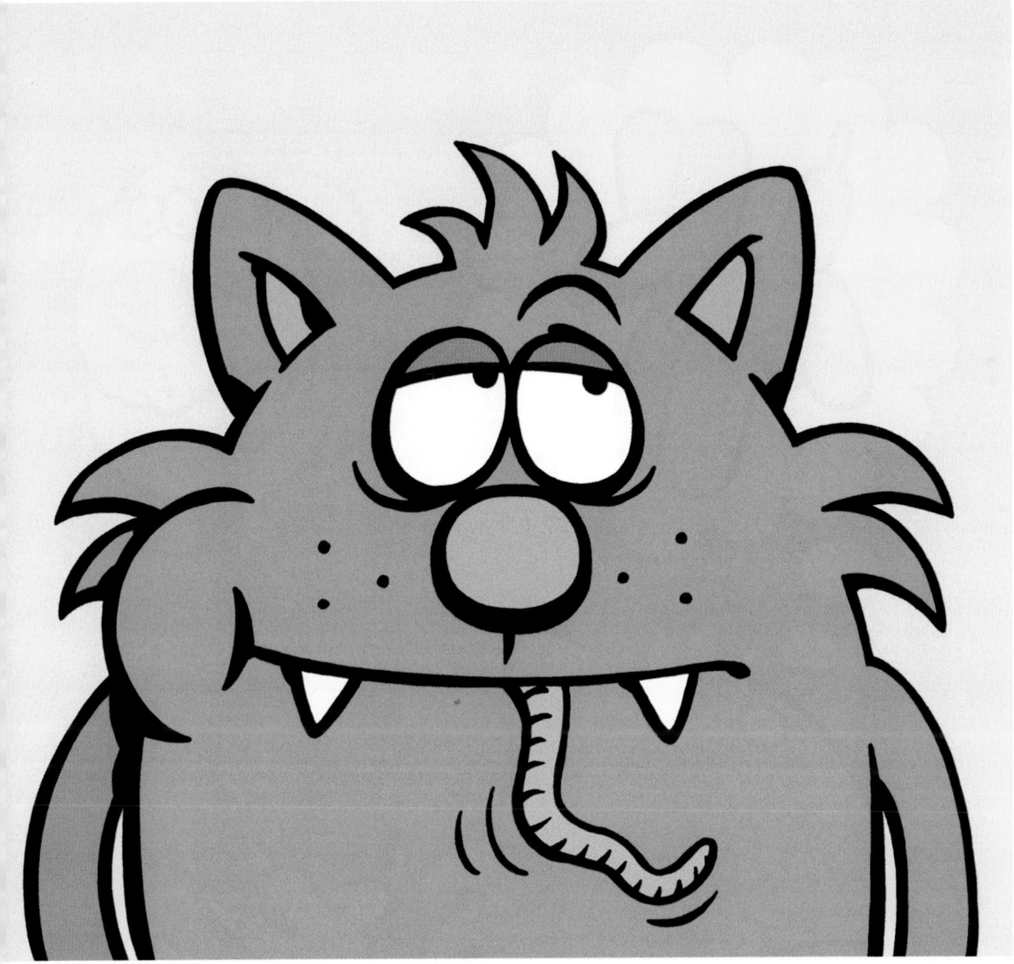

Ratachewy

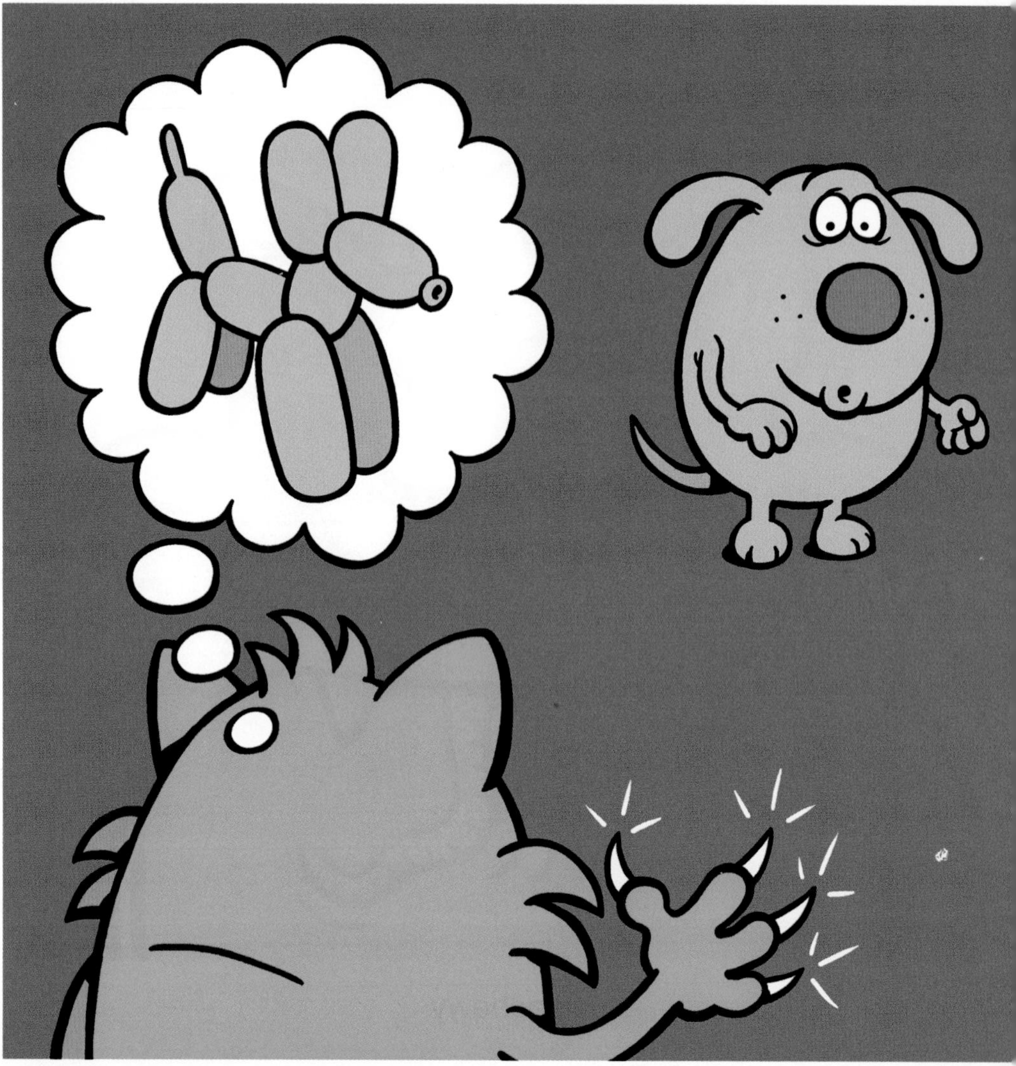

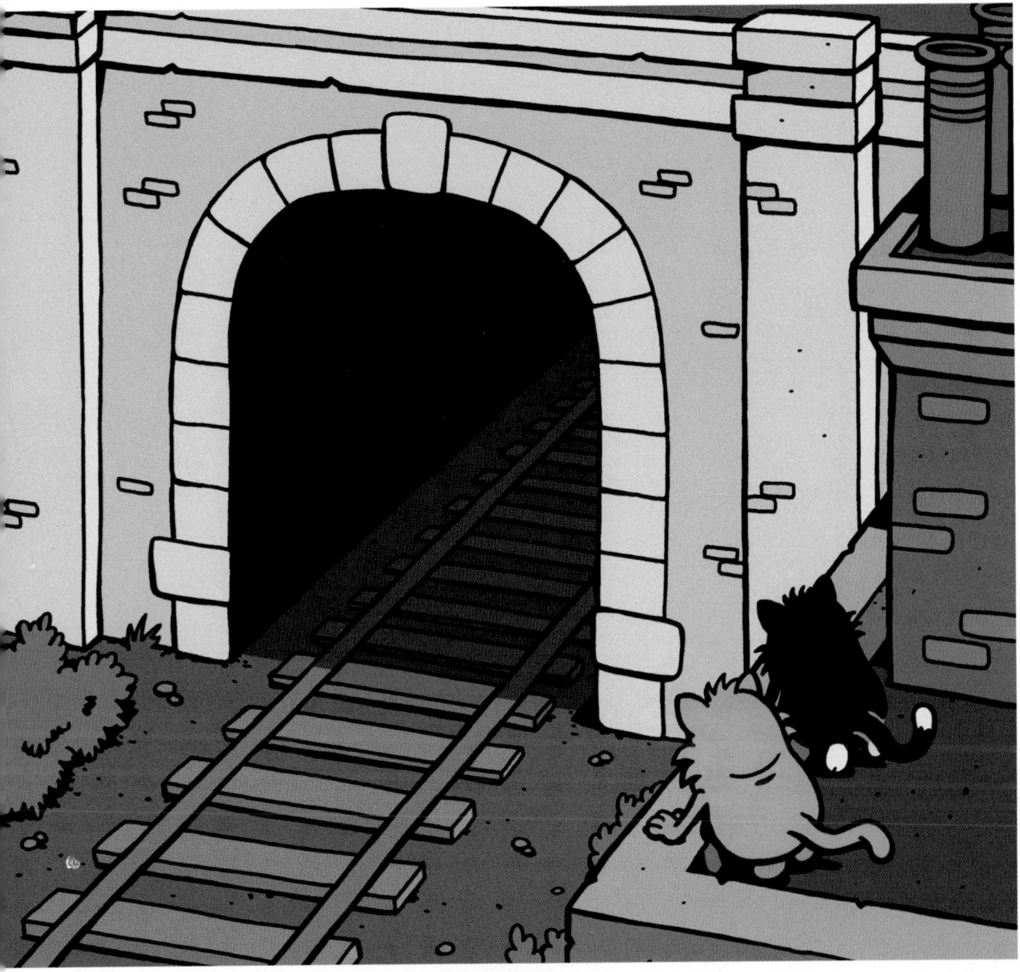

"They must have some big mice around here."

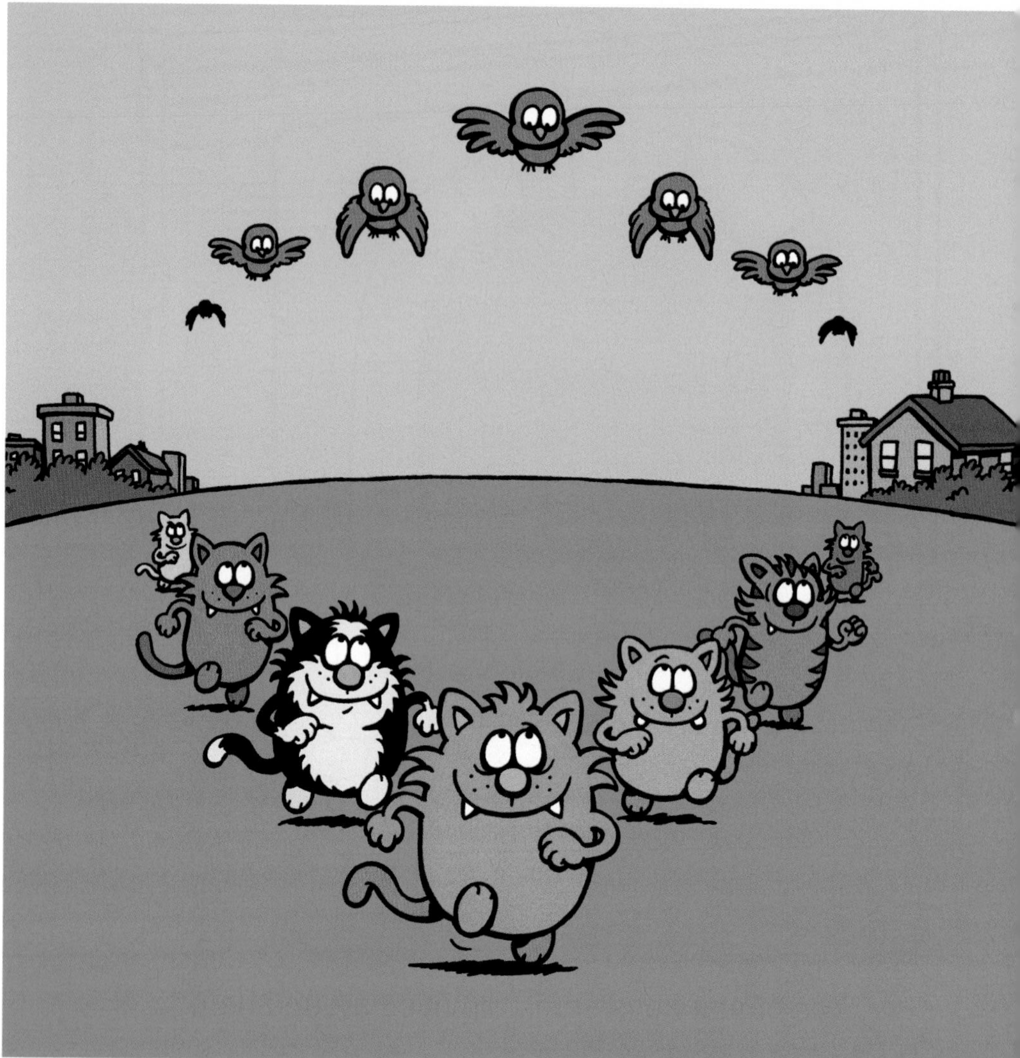

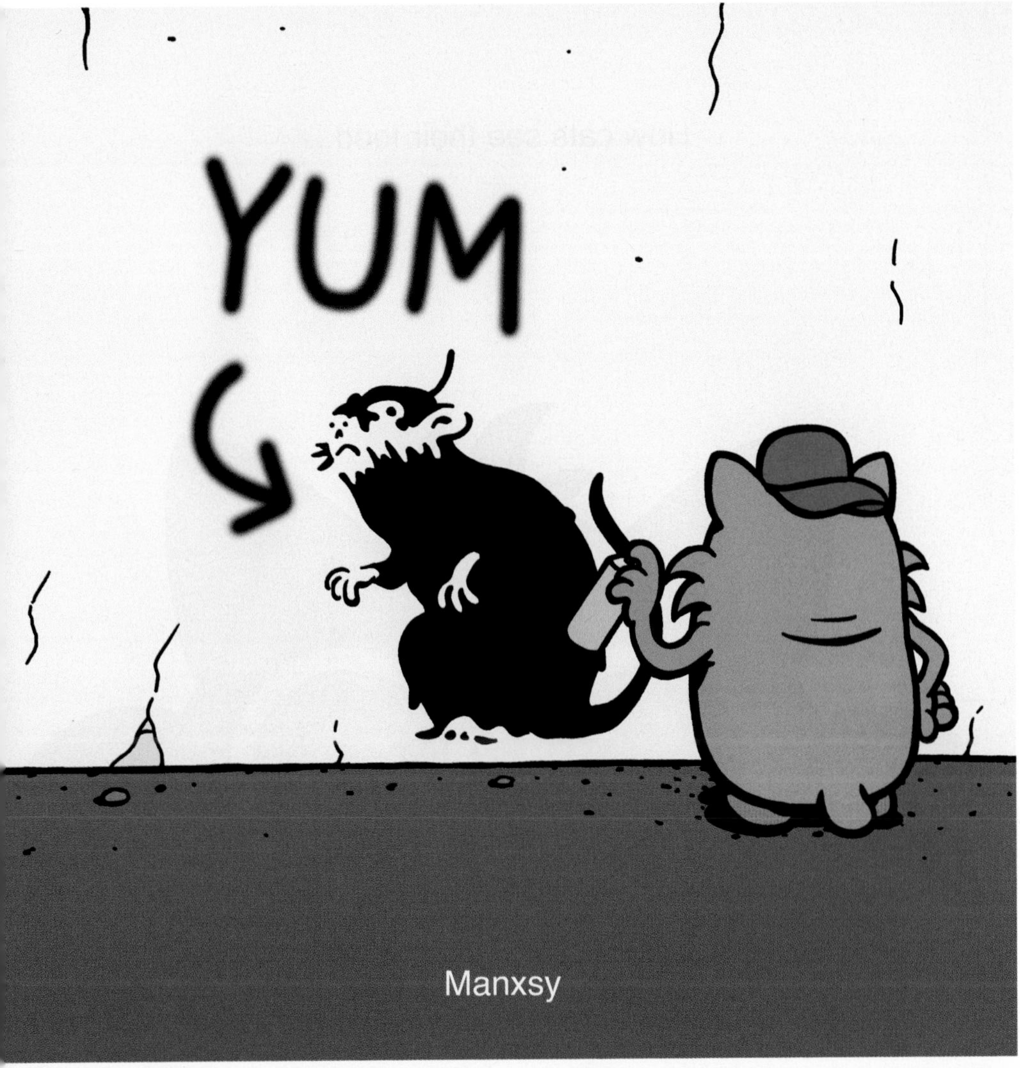
YUM

Manxsy

How cats see their food...

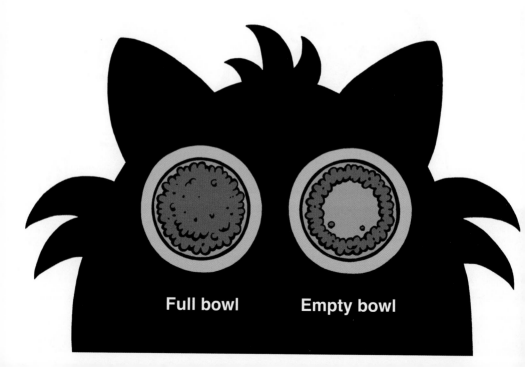

Full bowl   **Empty bowl**

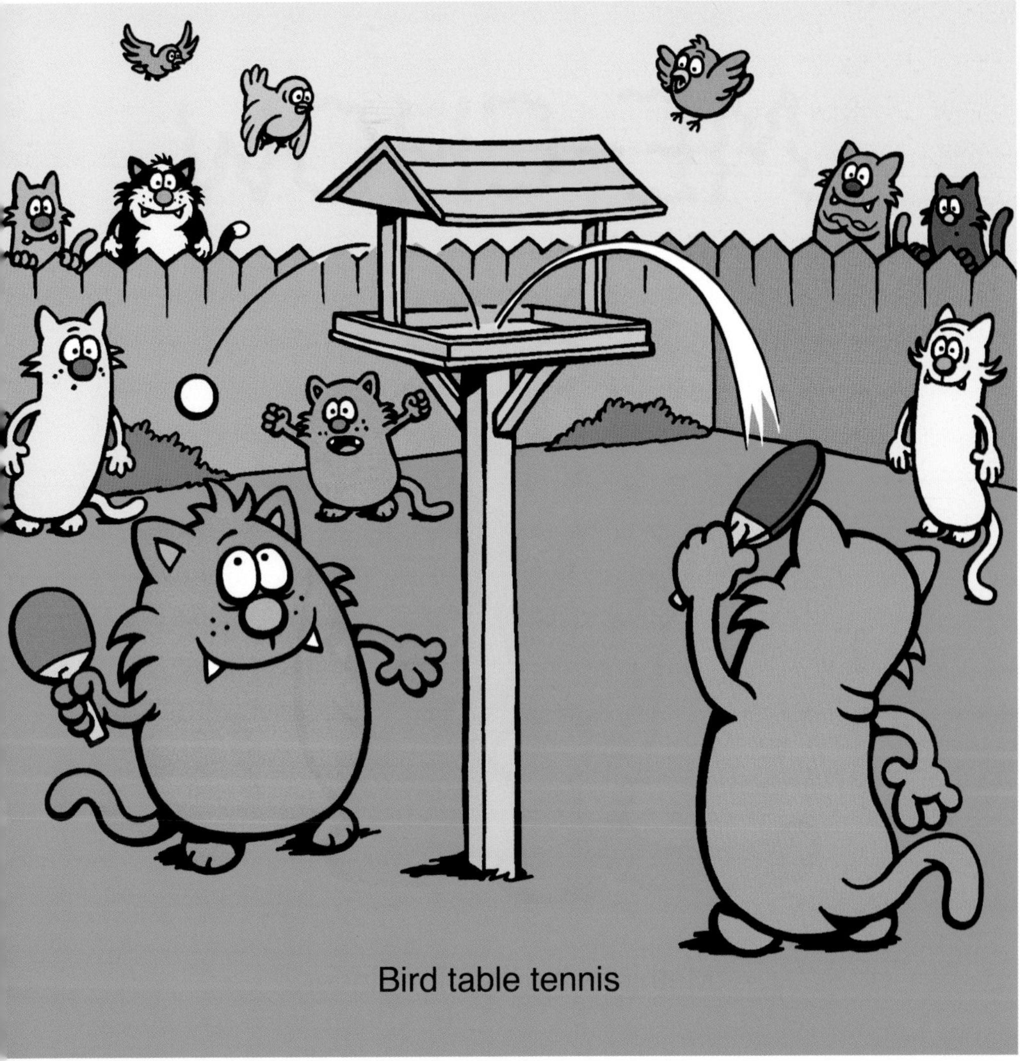

Bird table tennis

ME~CHOW

"Methinks it's time for dinner."

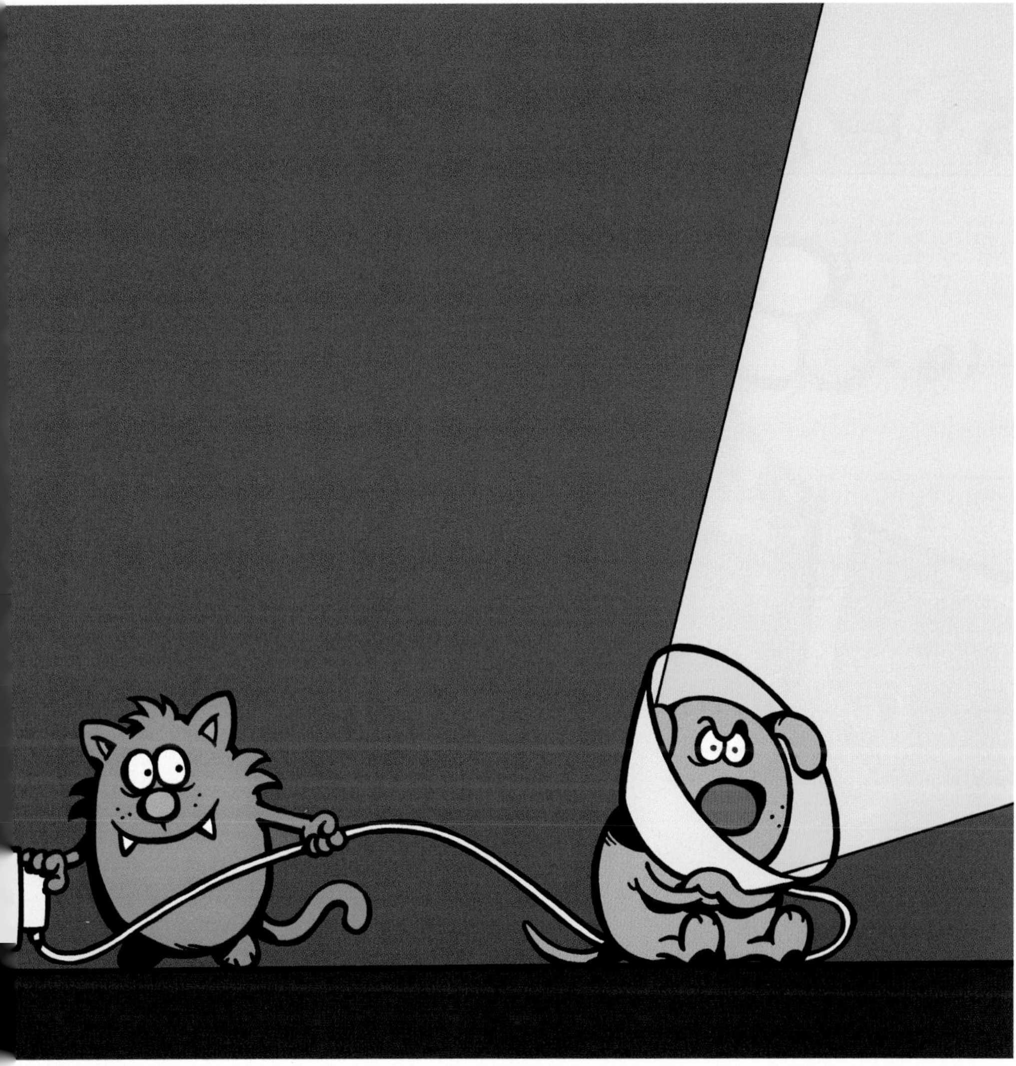

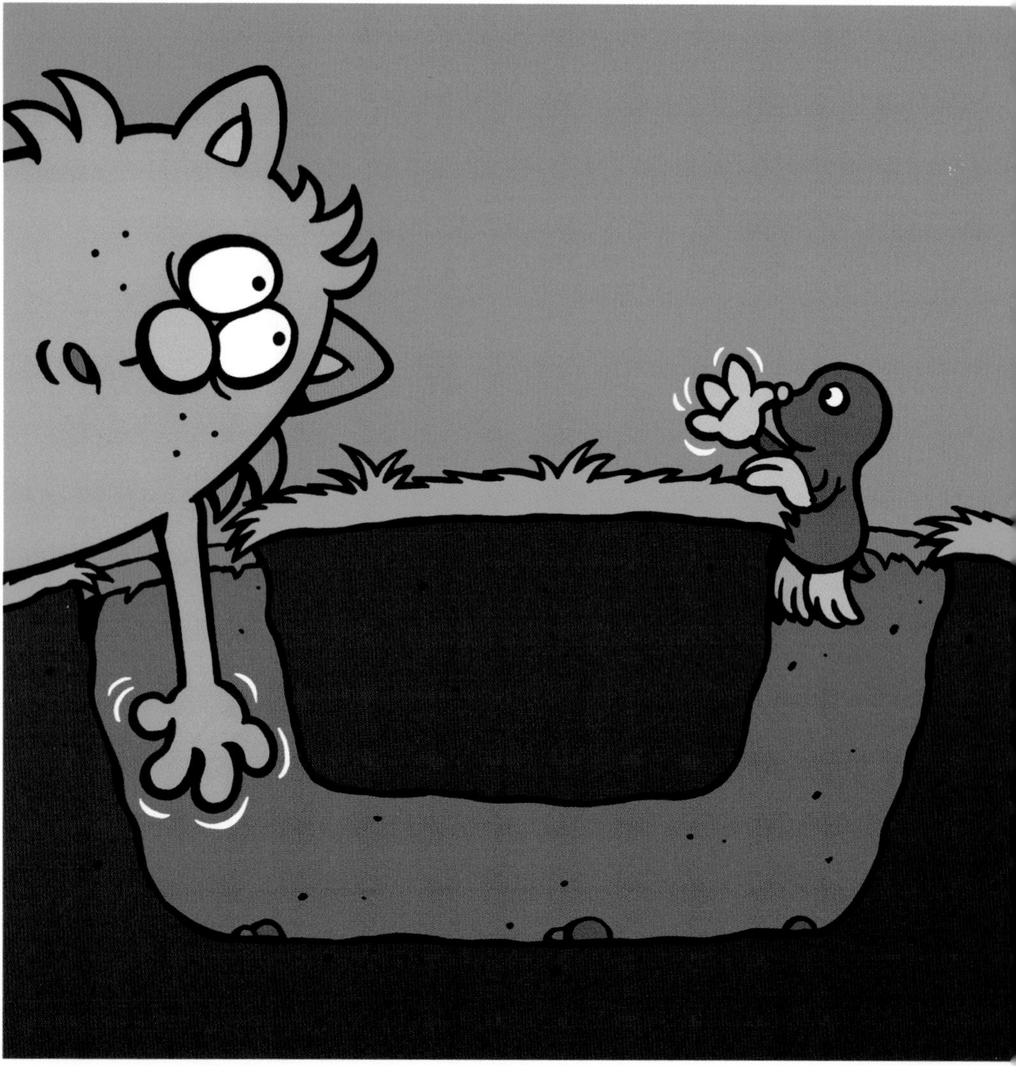

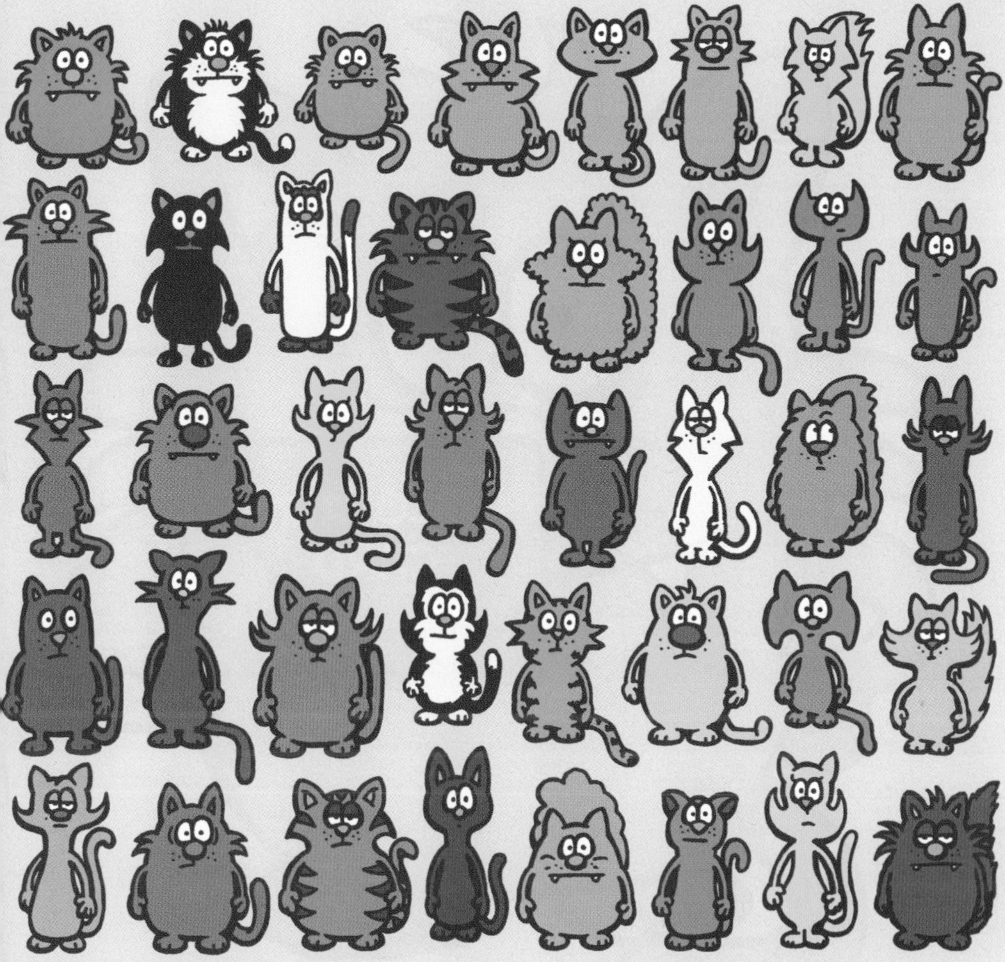

Crazy cat lady wallpaper (Copy this page several thousand times and paste to all interior walls)

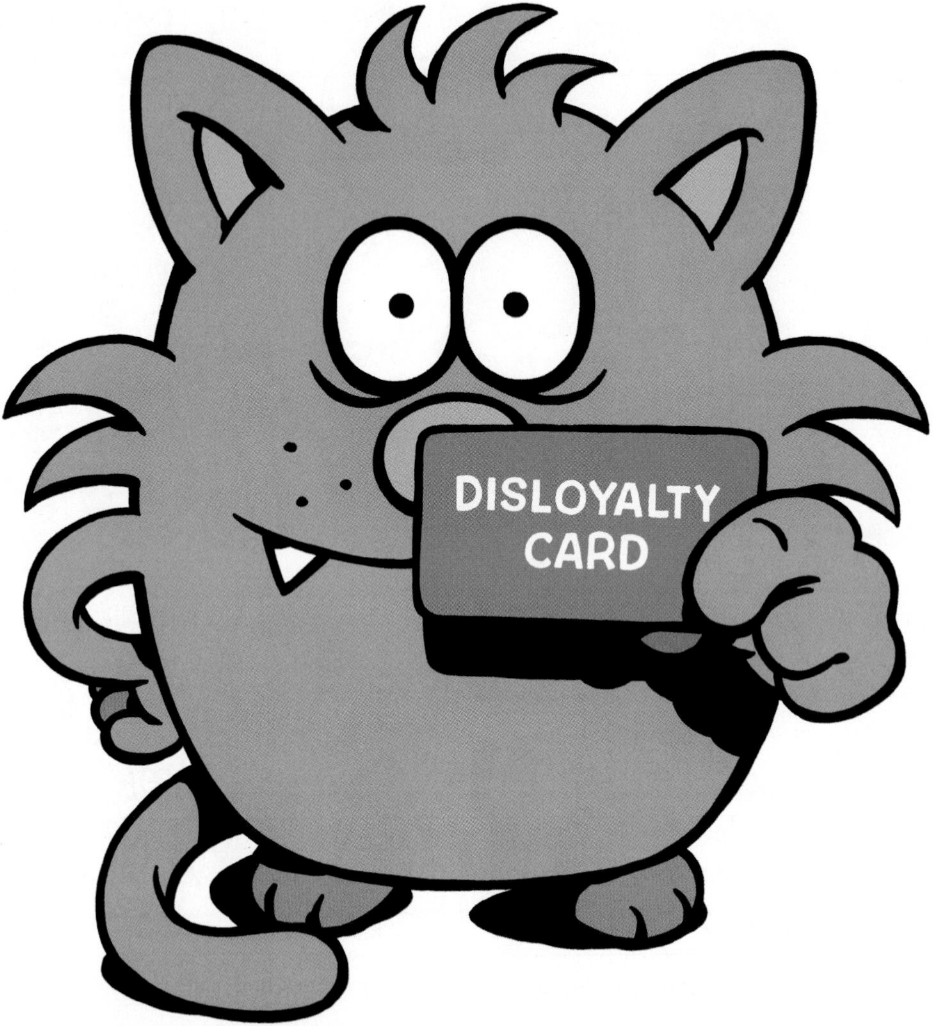
DISLOYALTY
CARD

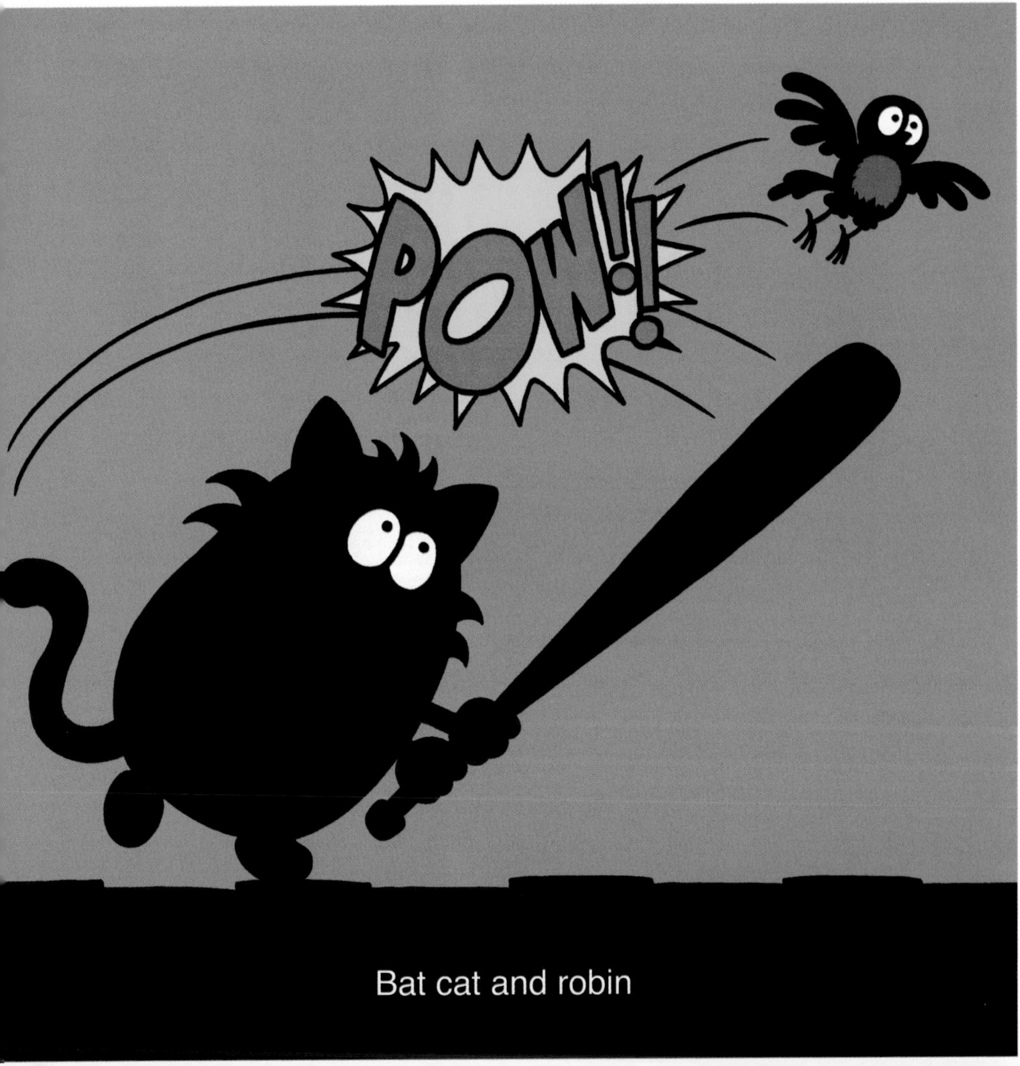
POW!!

Bat cat and robin

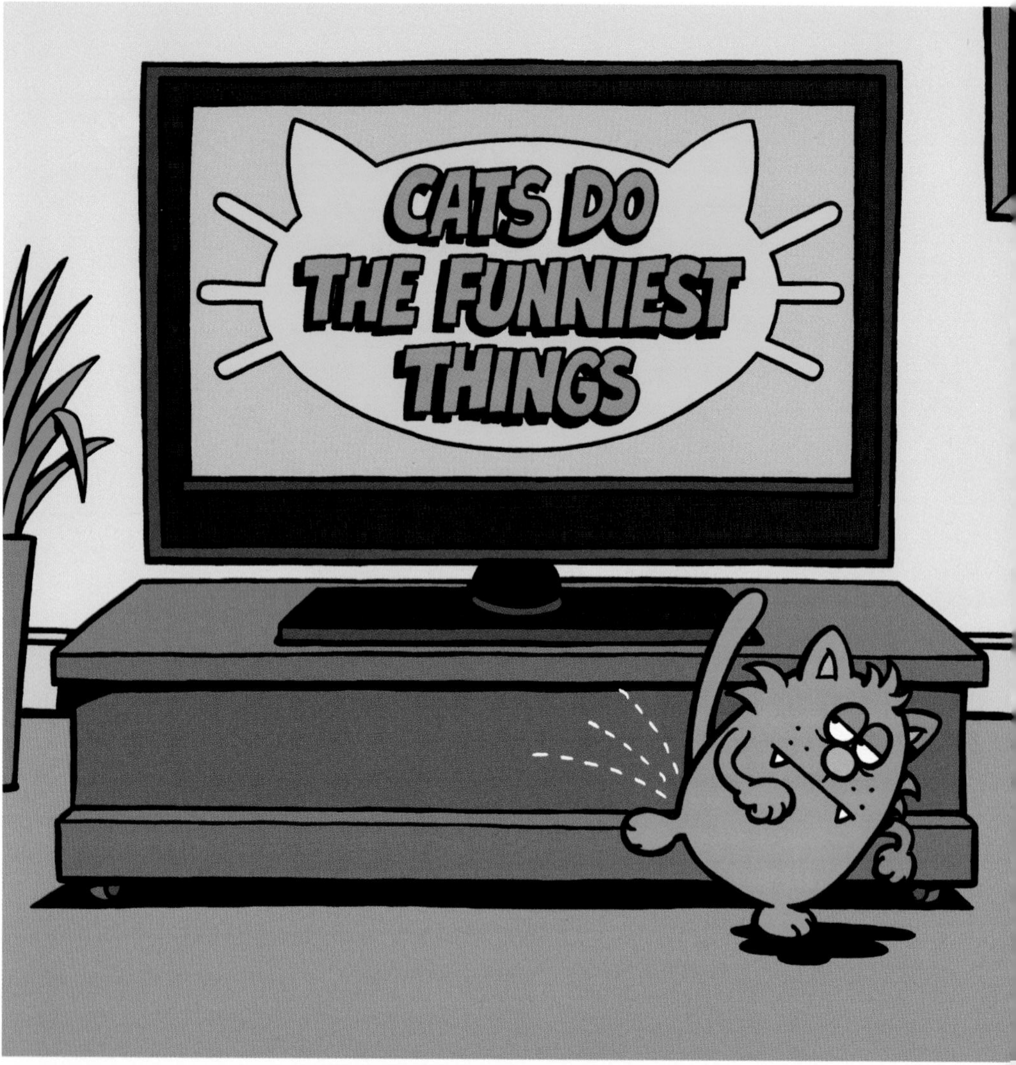
CATS DO
THE FUNNIEST
THINGS

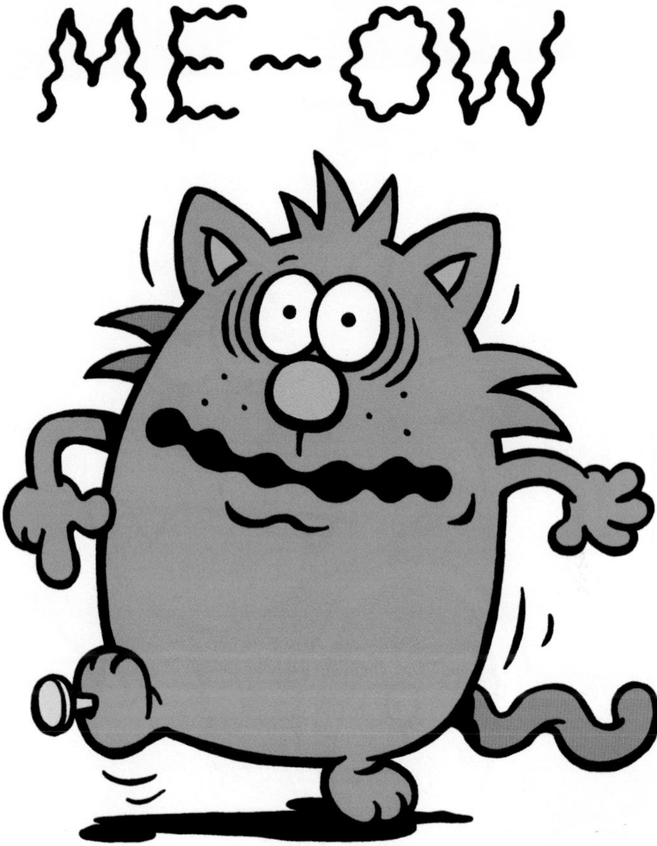
ME-OW

"This rather hurts."

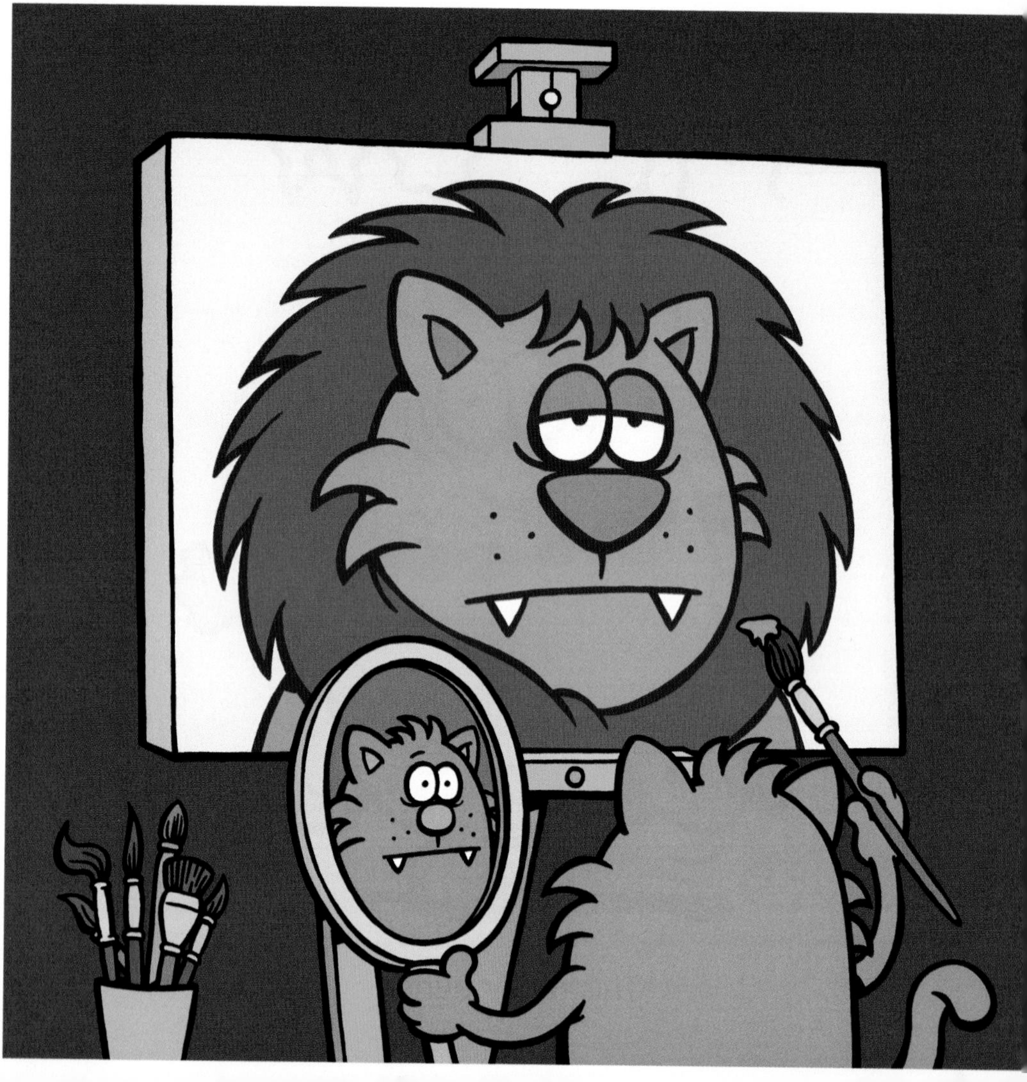

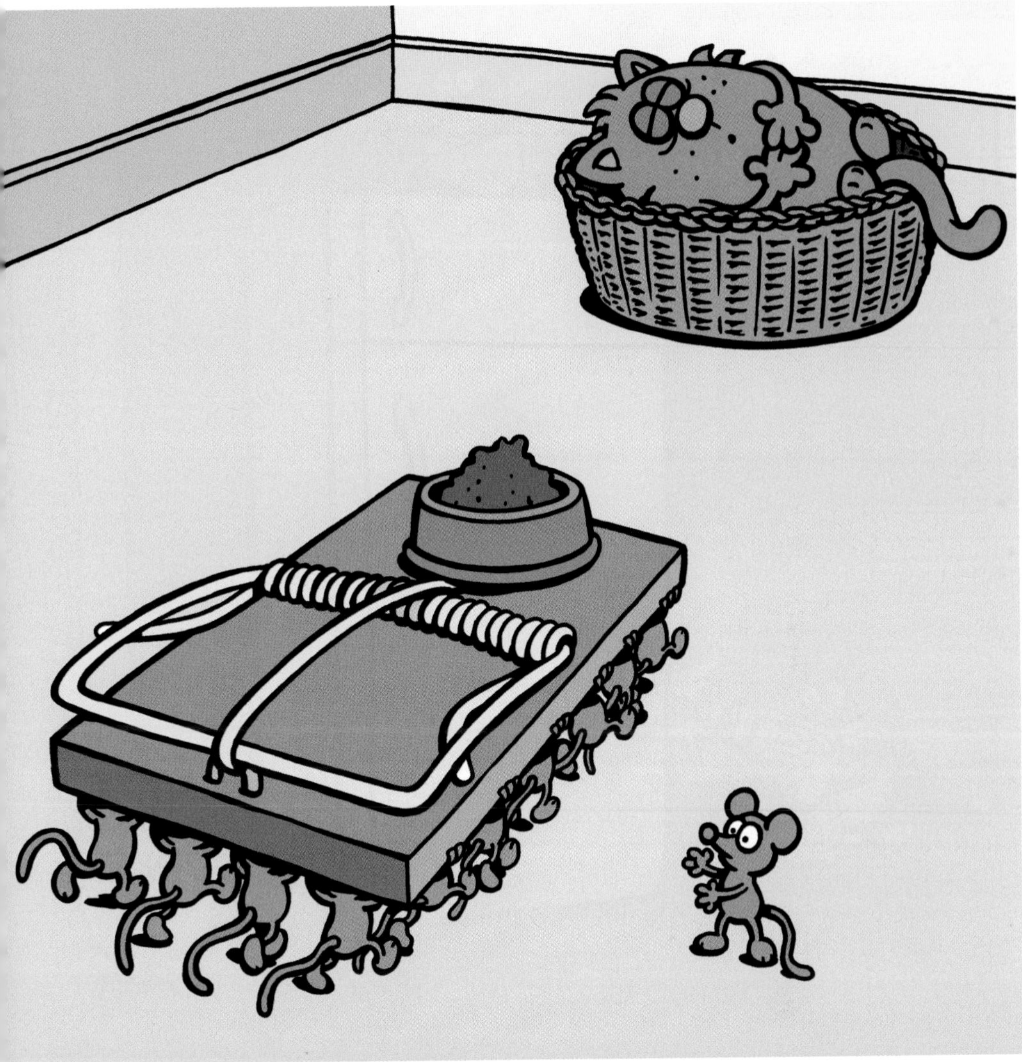

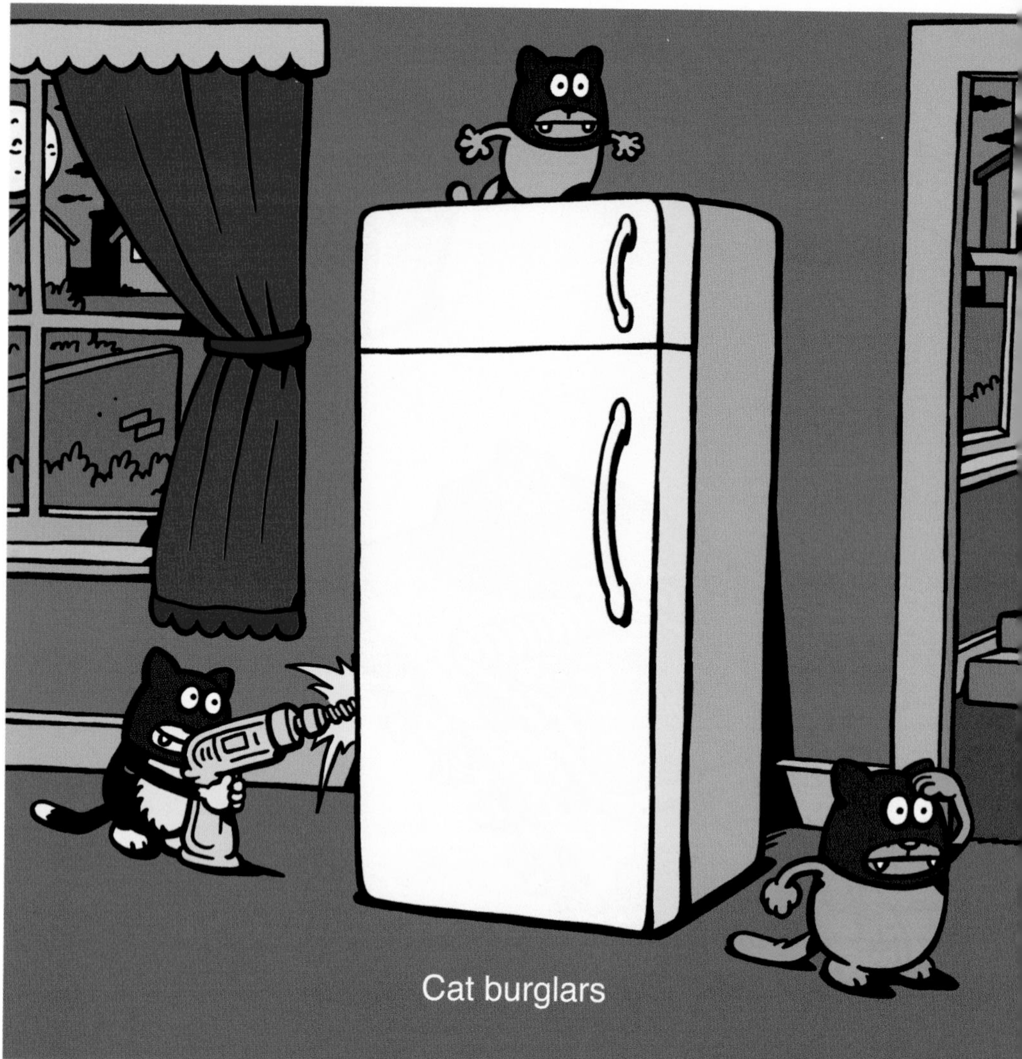

Cat burglars

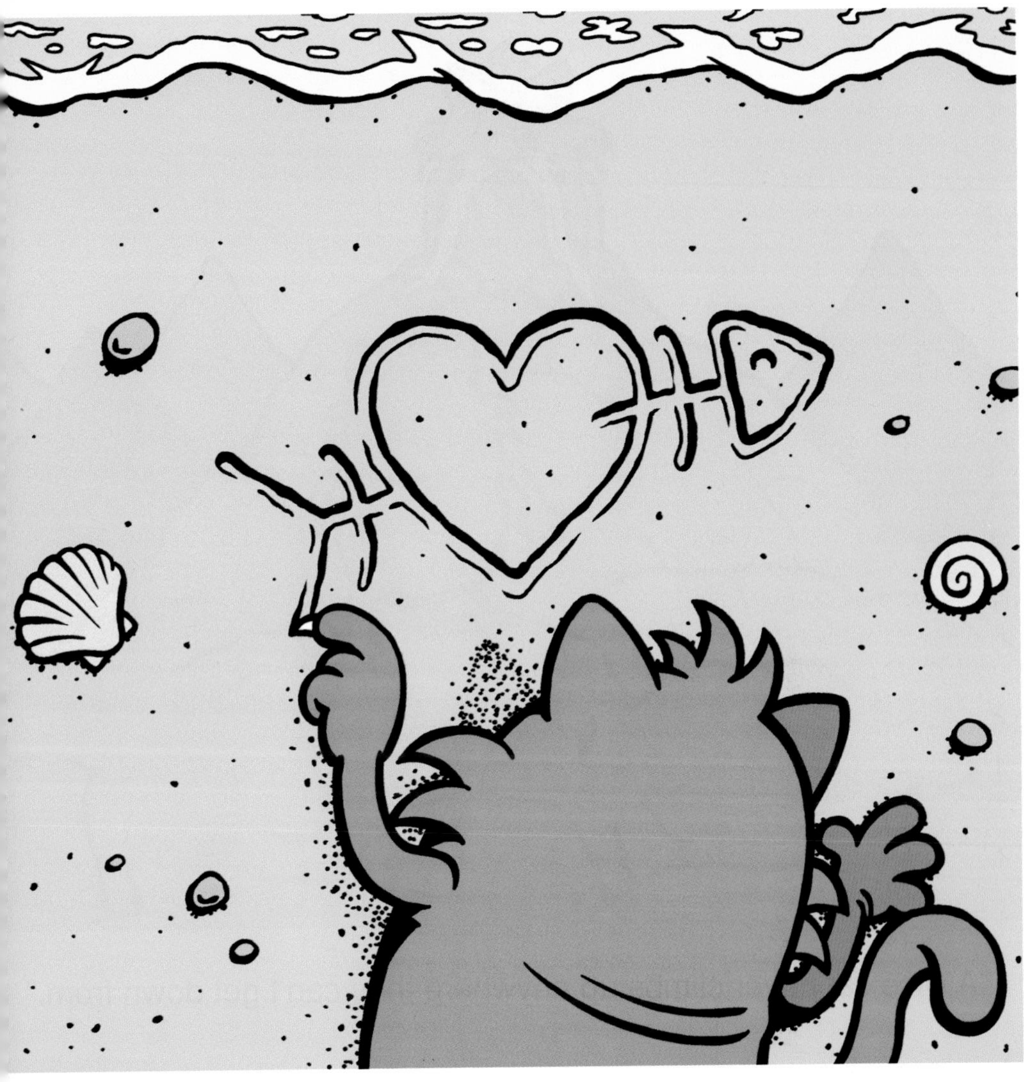

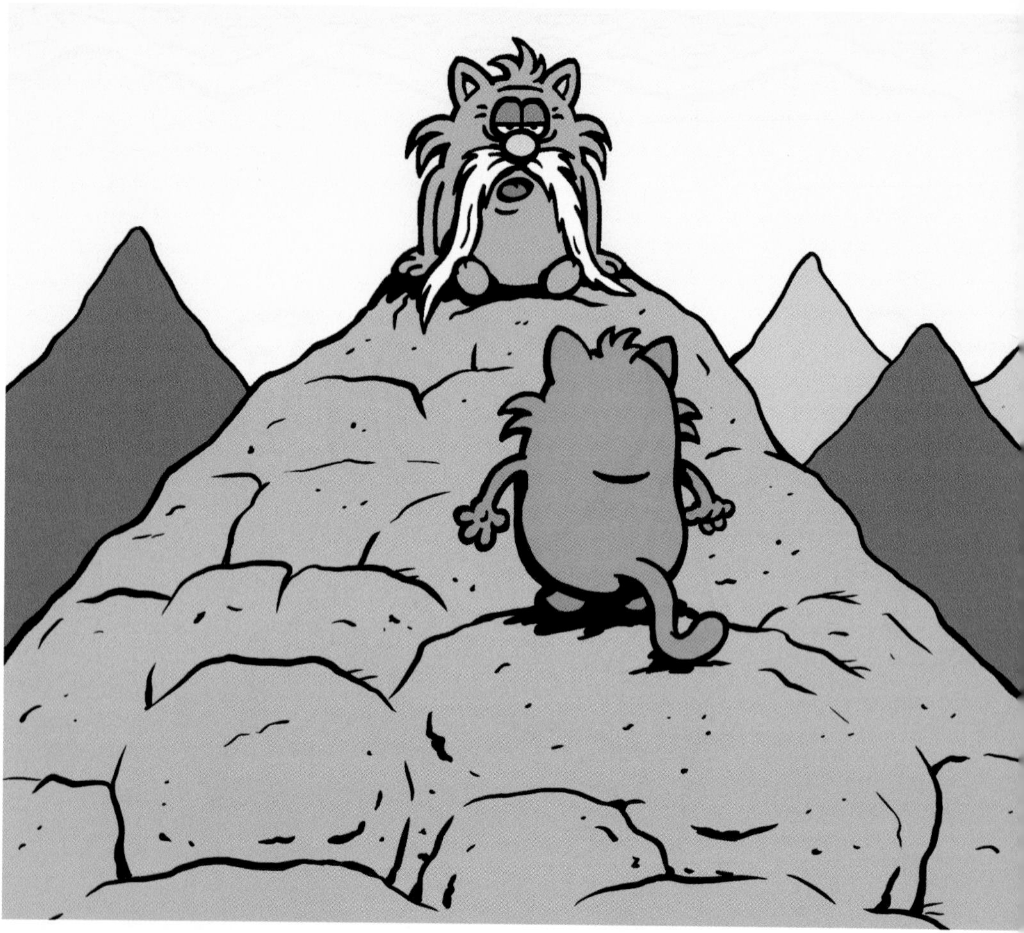

“A wise cat never climbs up anywhere they can’t get down from.”

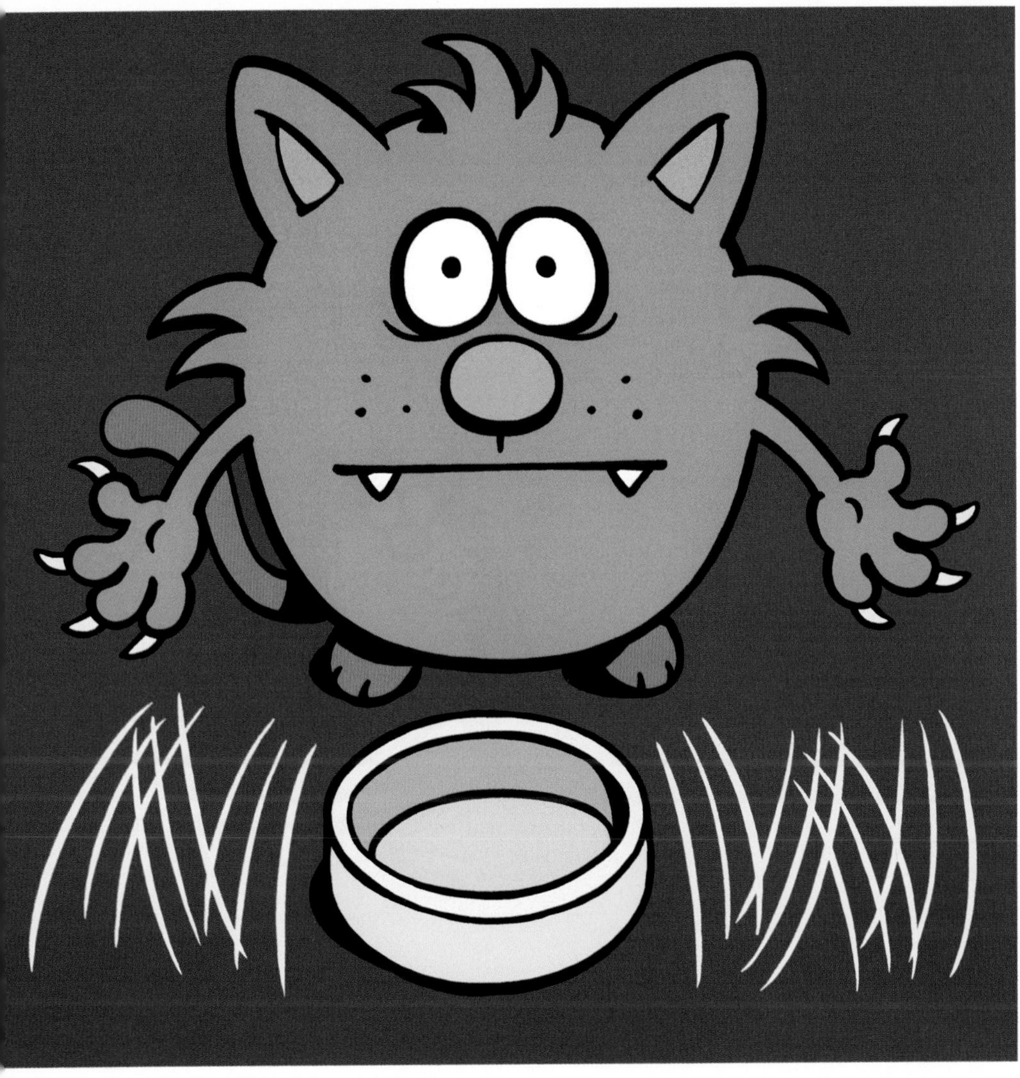

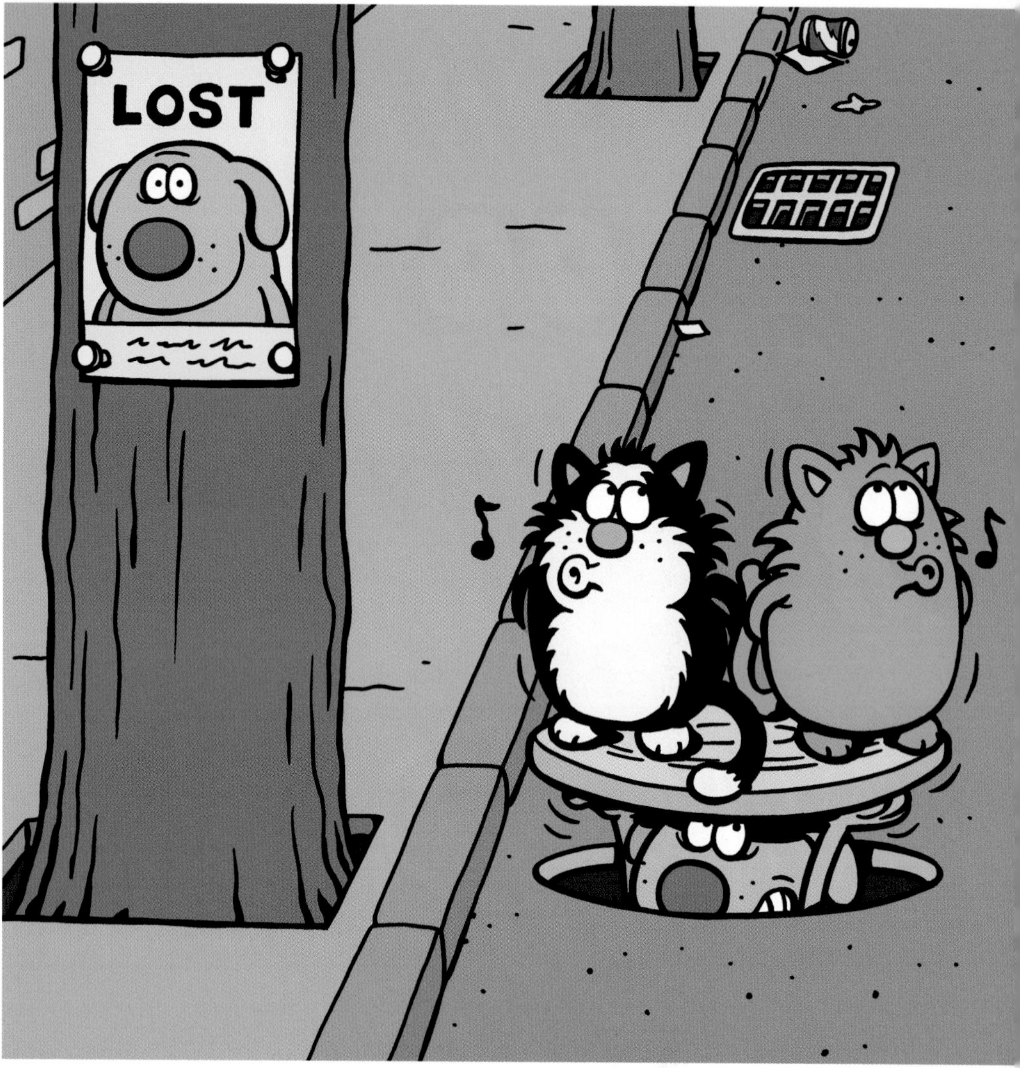
LOST

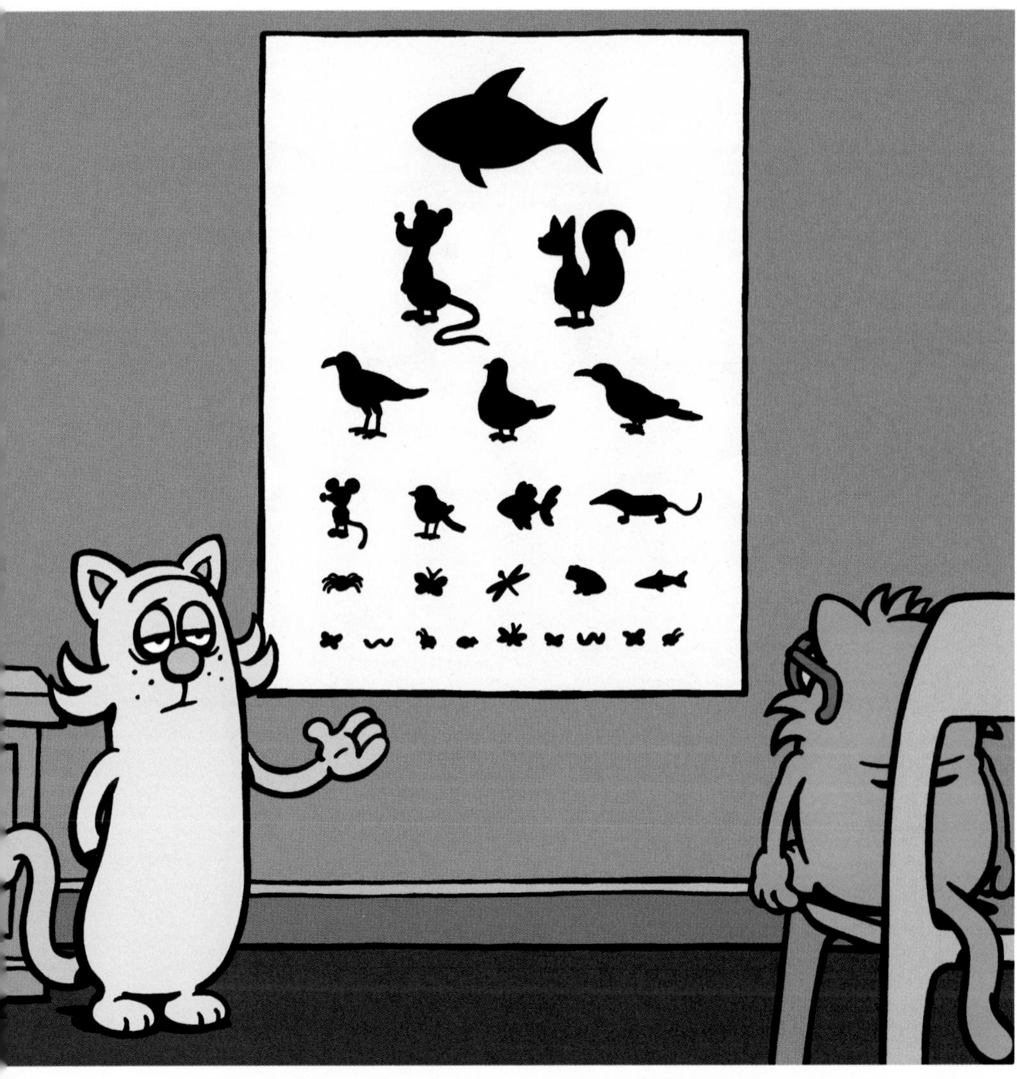

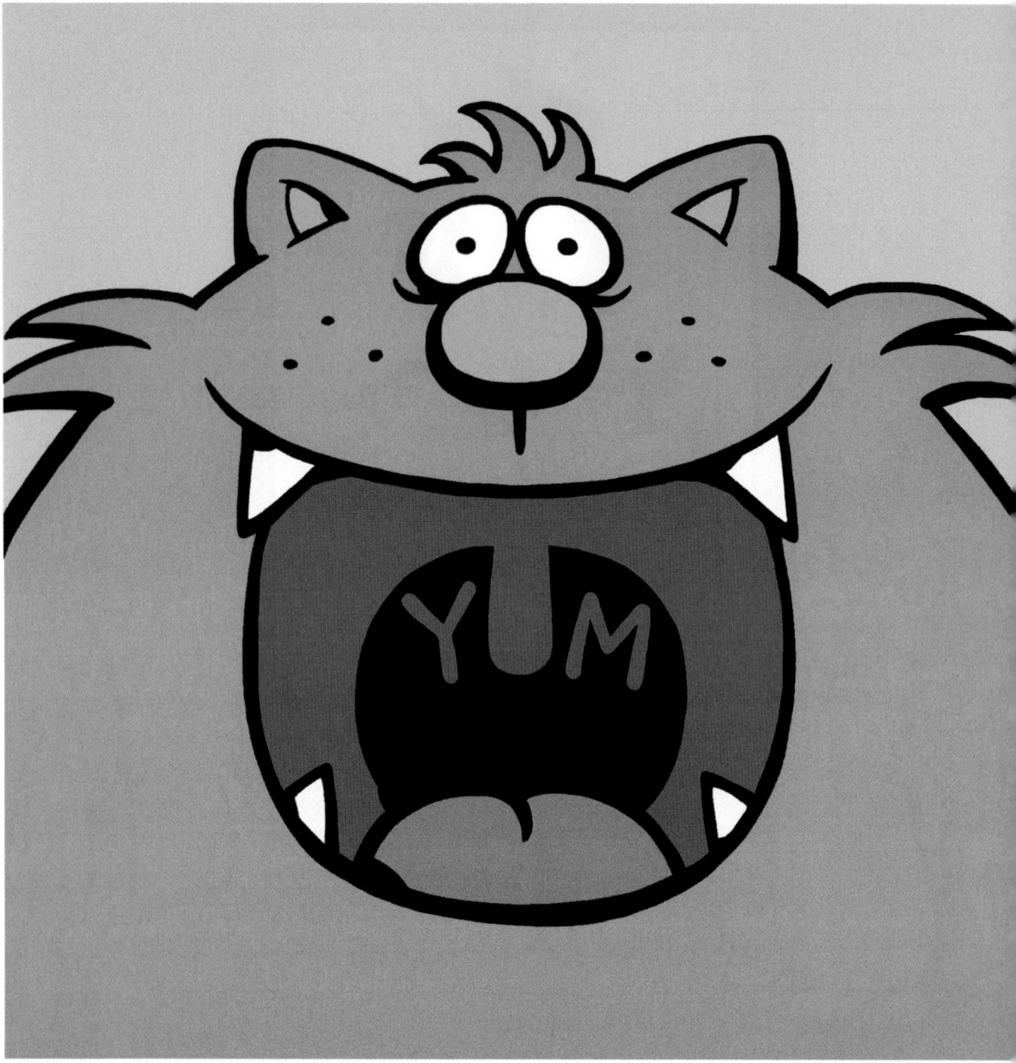
YUM

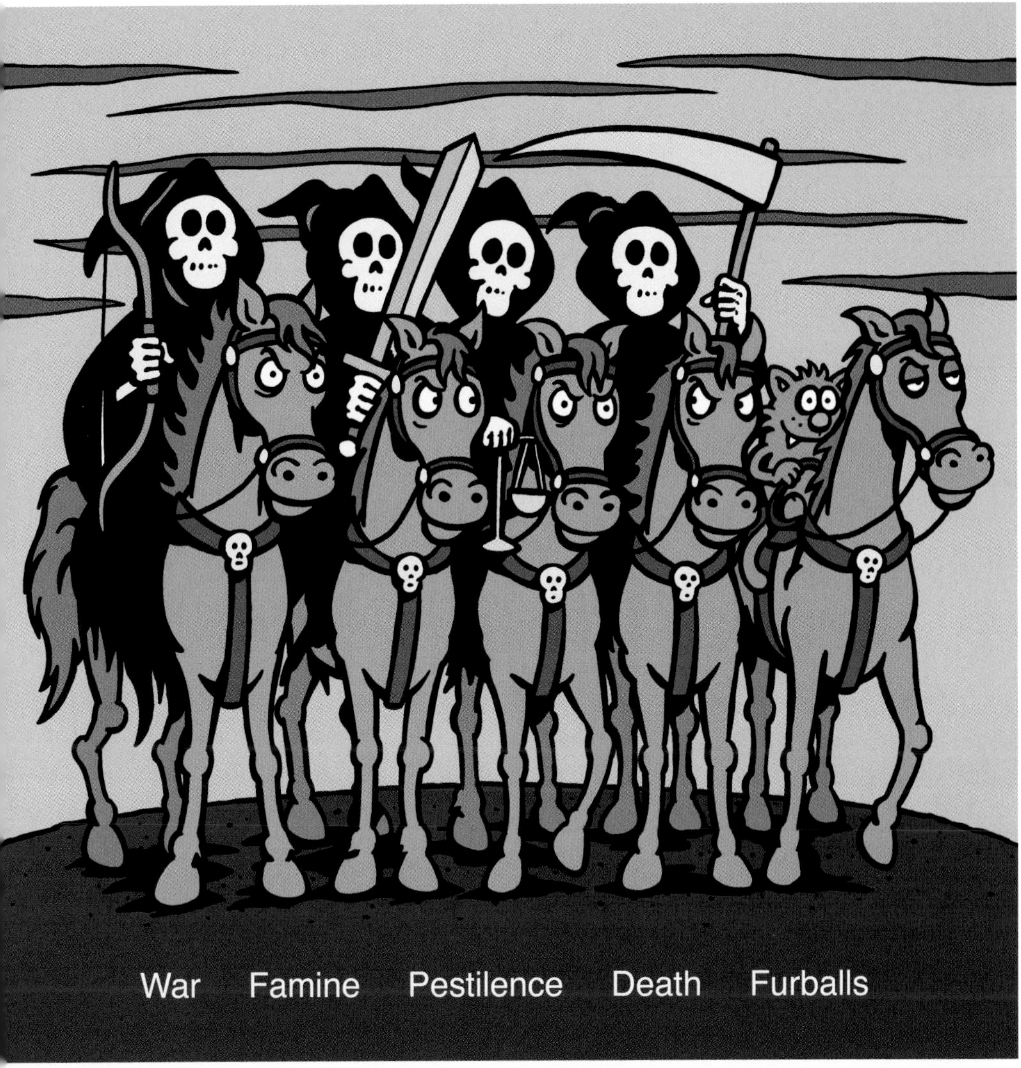
War
Famine
Pestilence
Death
Furballs

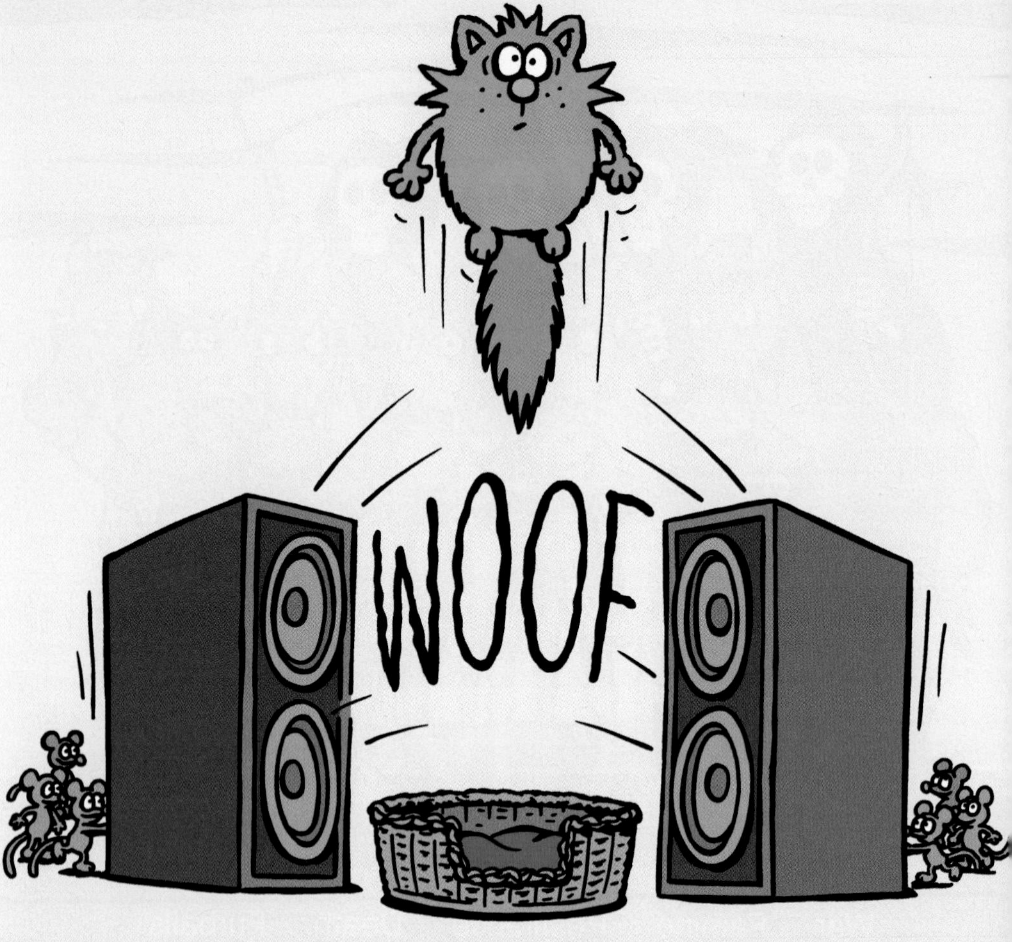
WOOF

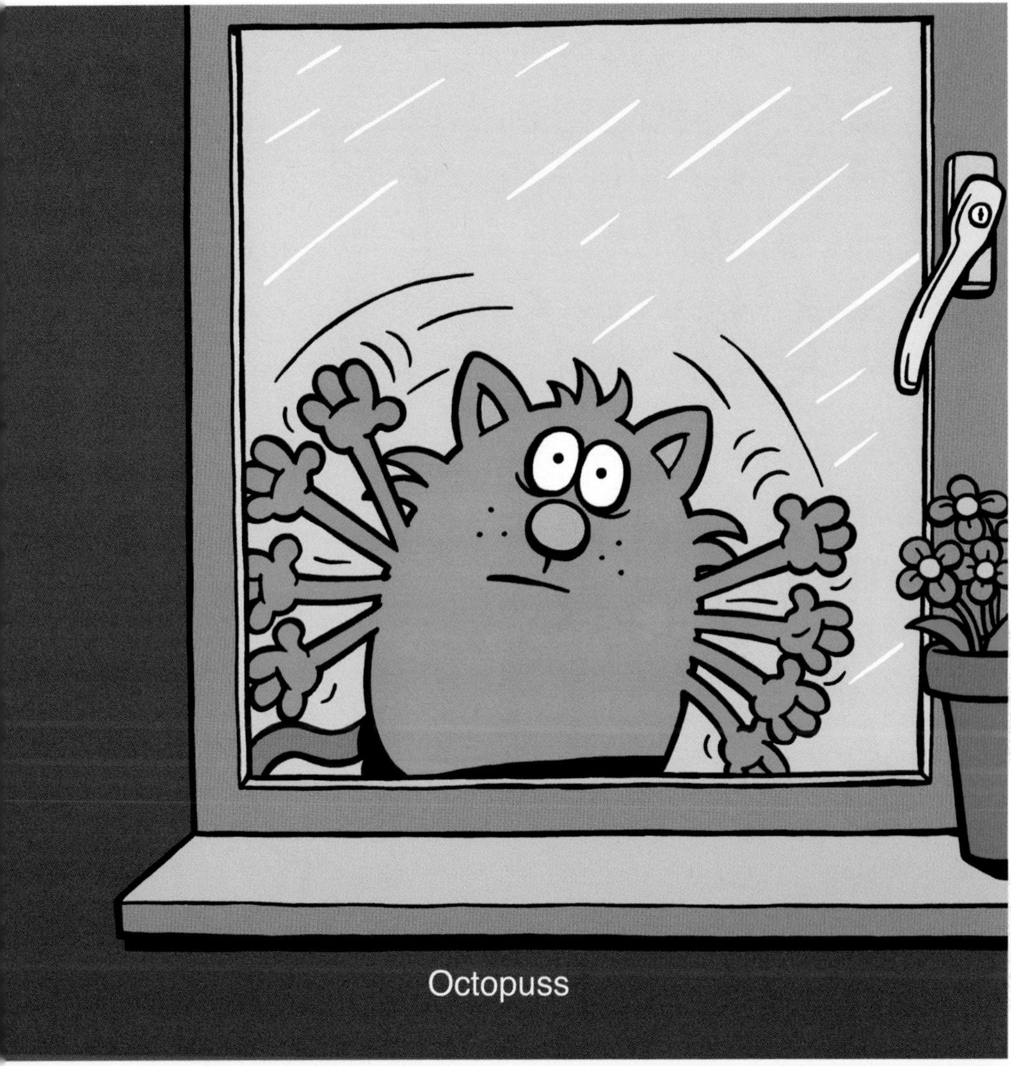

Octopuss

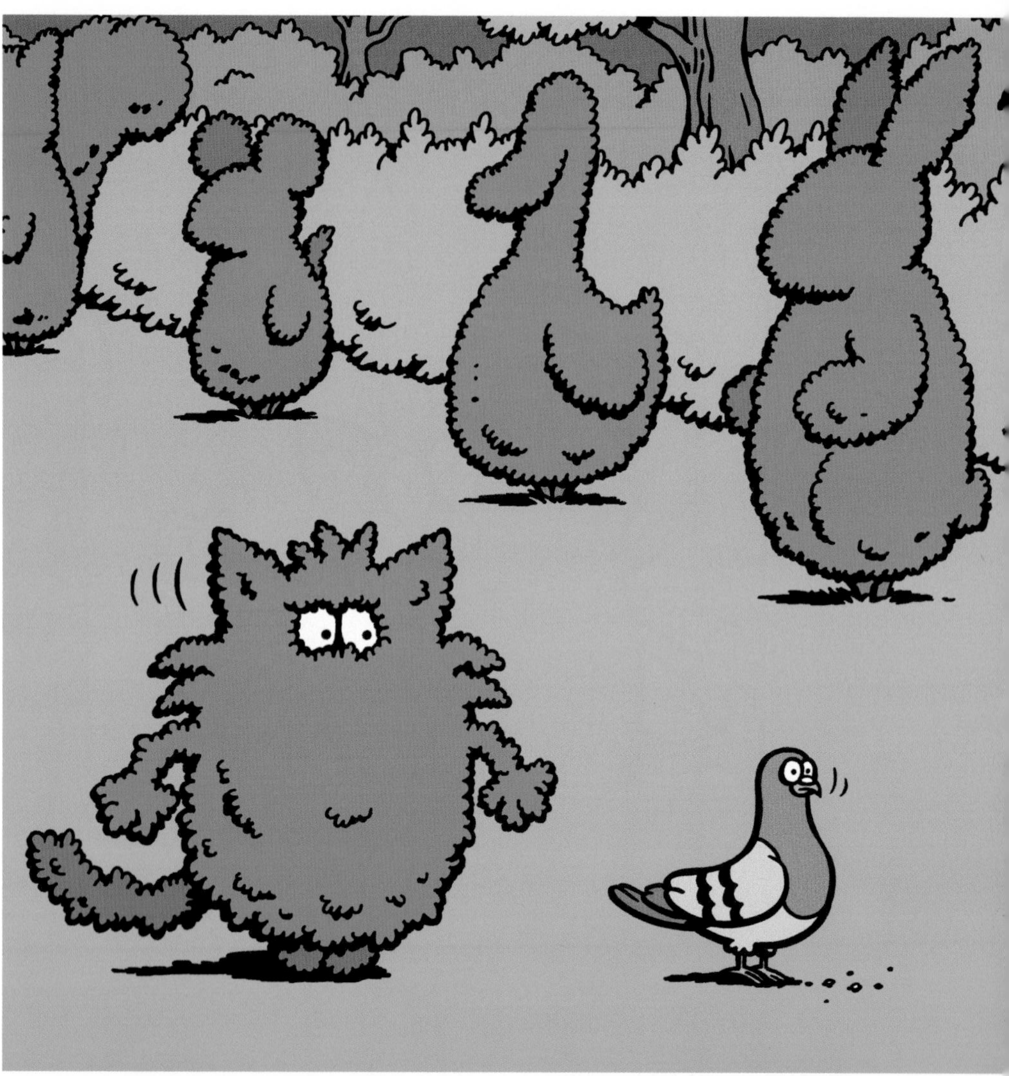

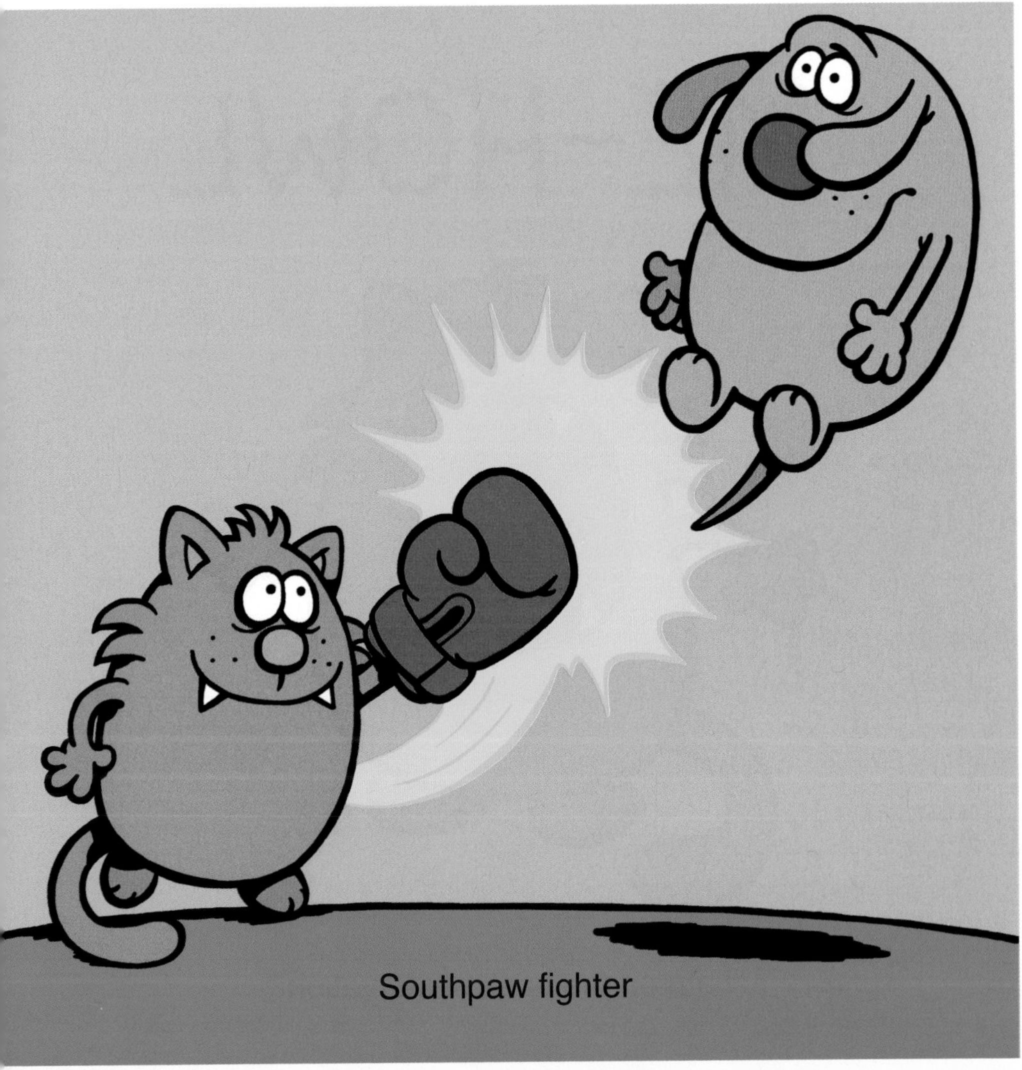

Southpaw fighter

ME~HOWL

"I am on the brink of starvation."

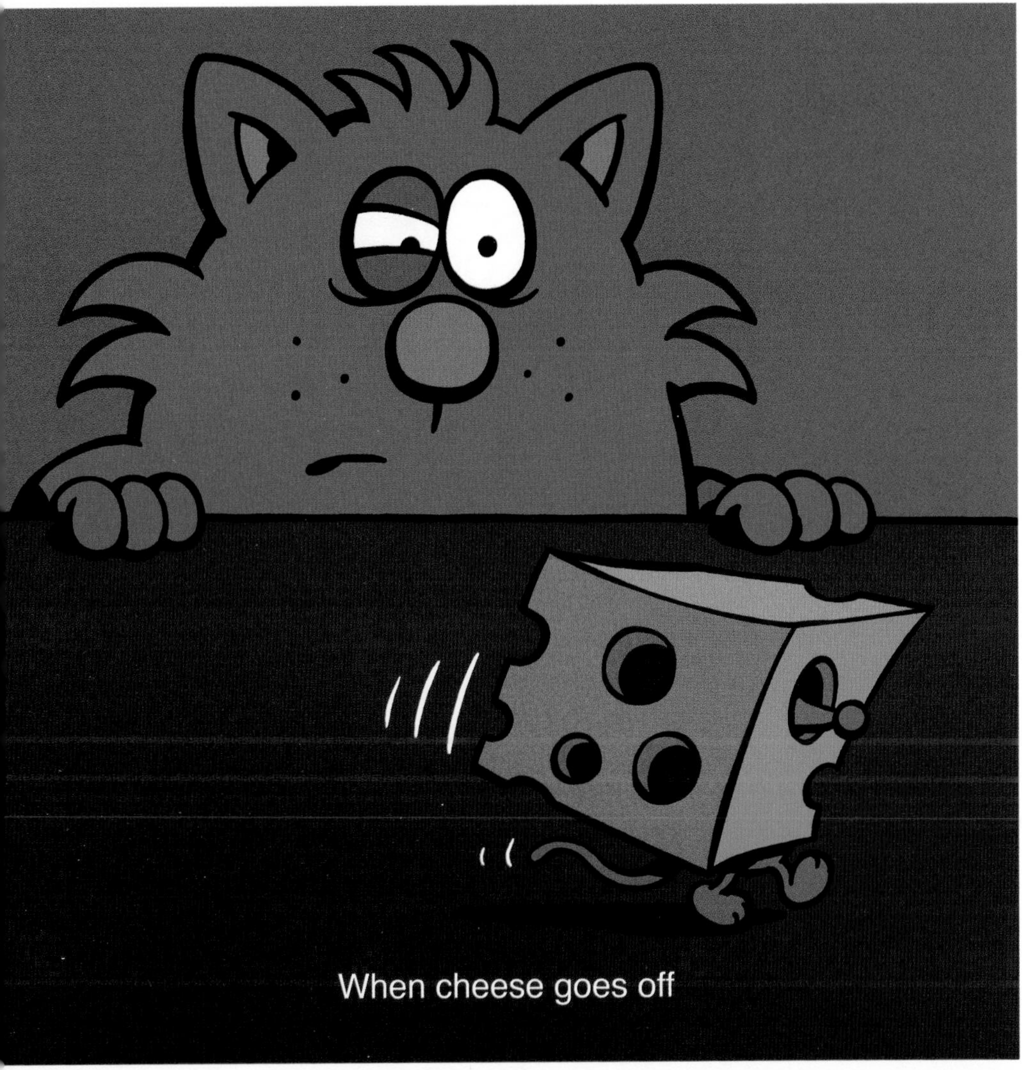

When cheese goes off

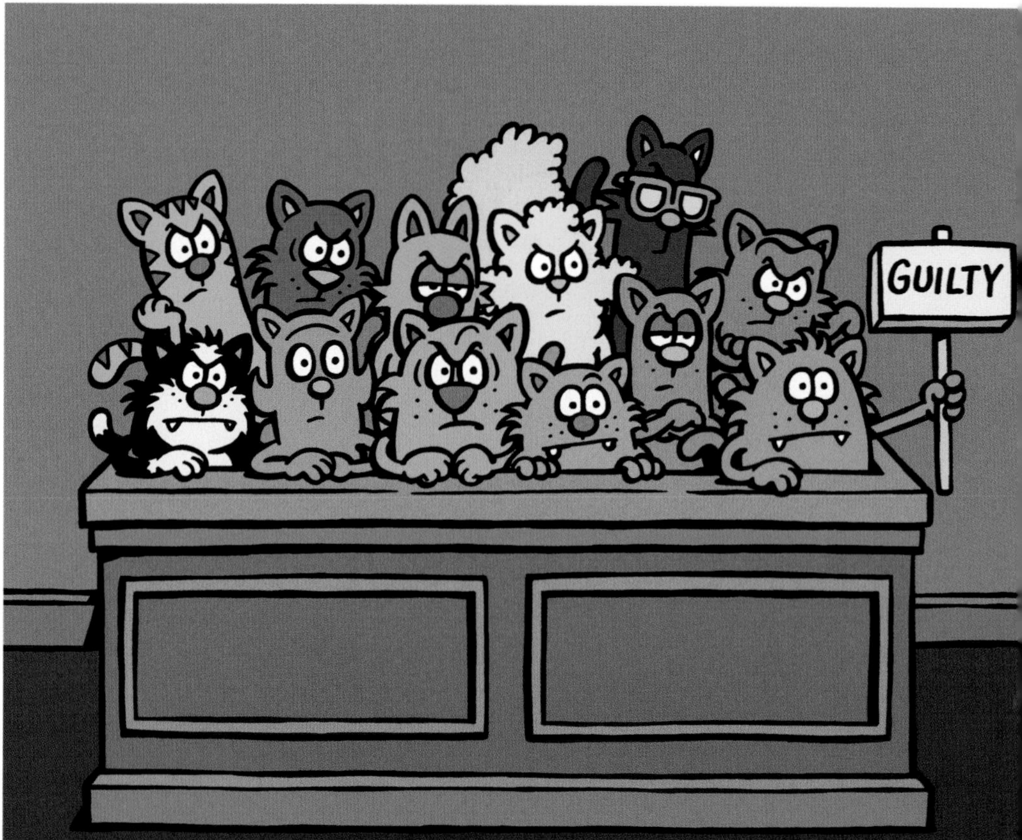
GUILTY

Sheep dog trials

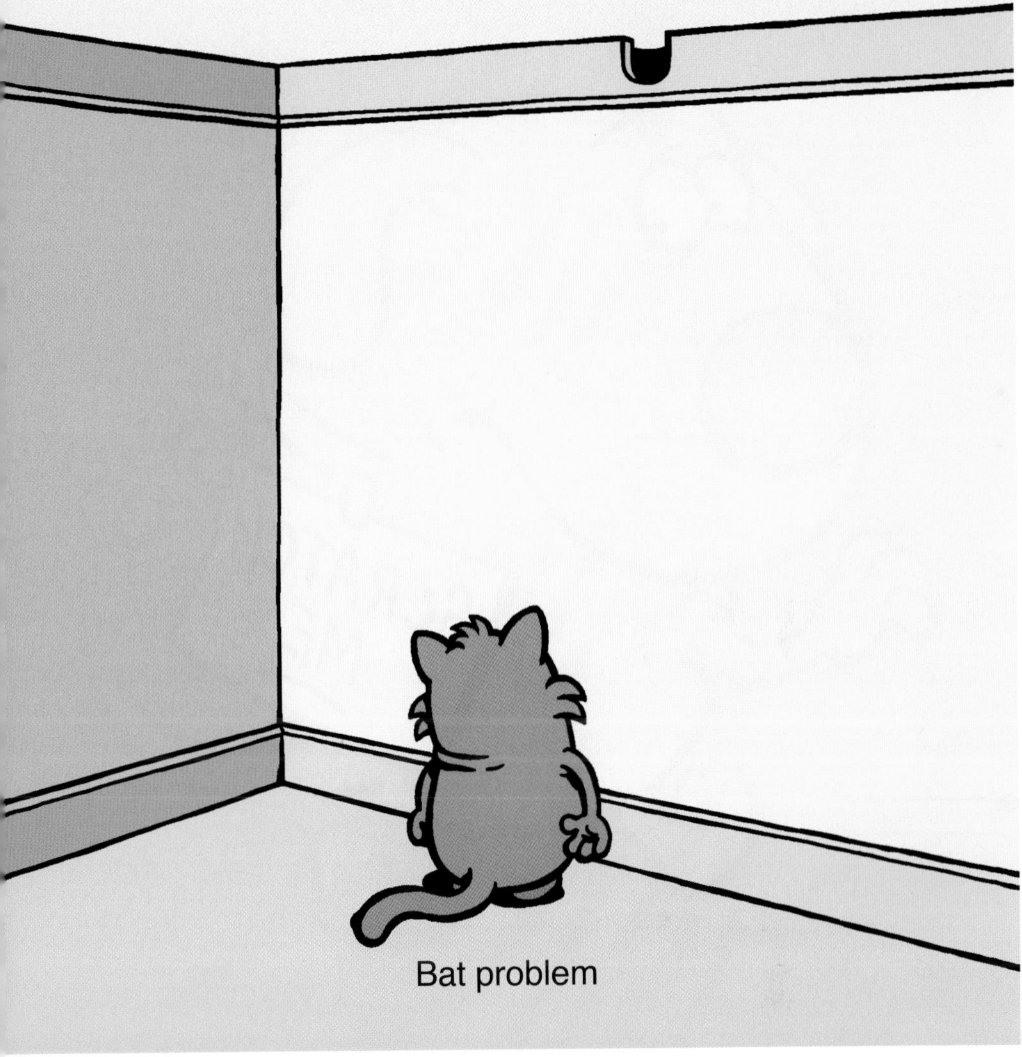

Bat problem

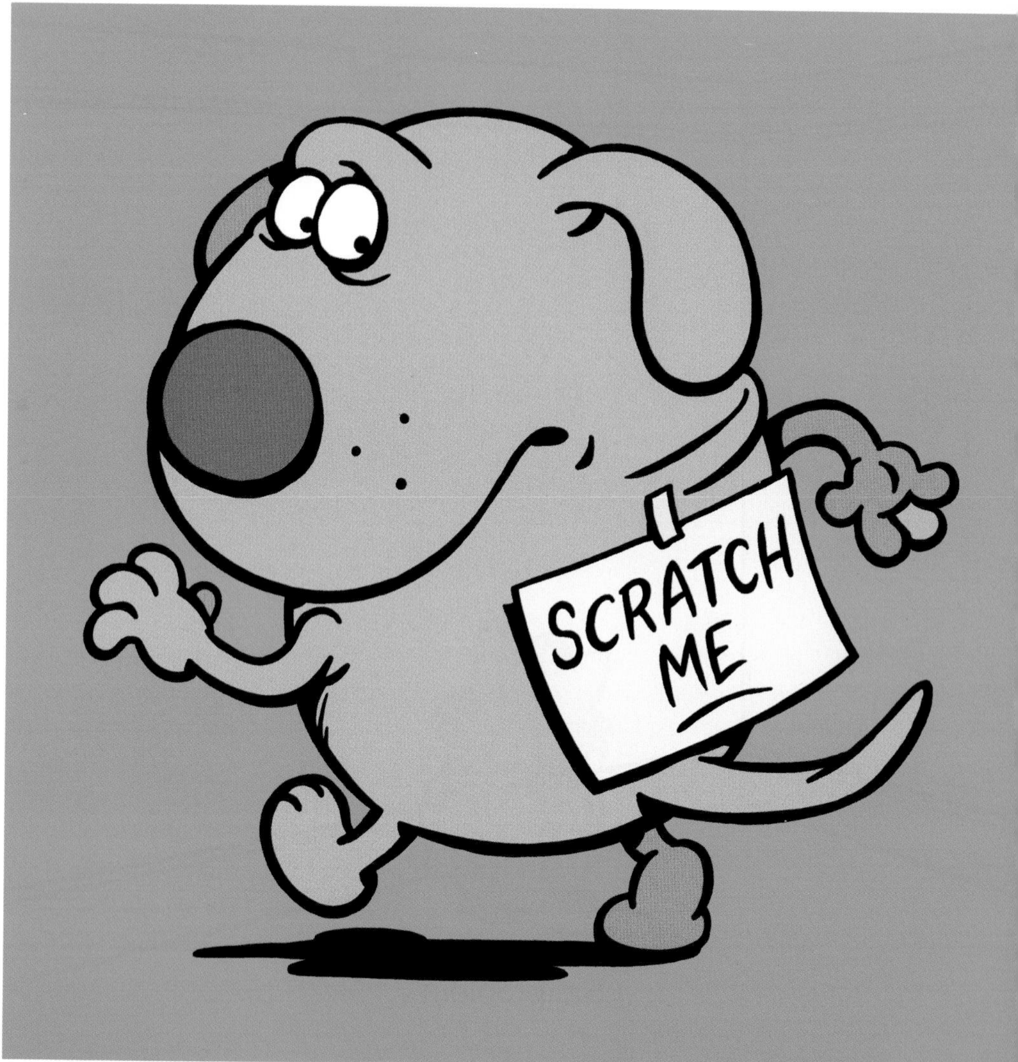
SCRATCH
ME

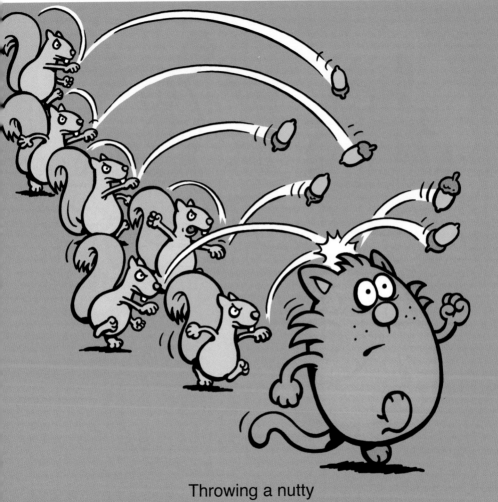

Throwing a nutty

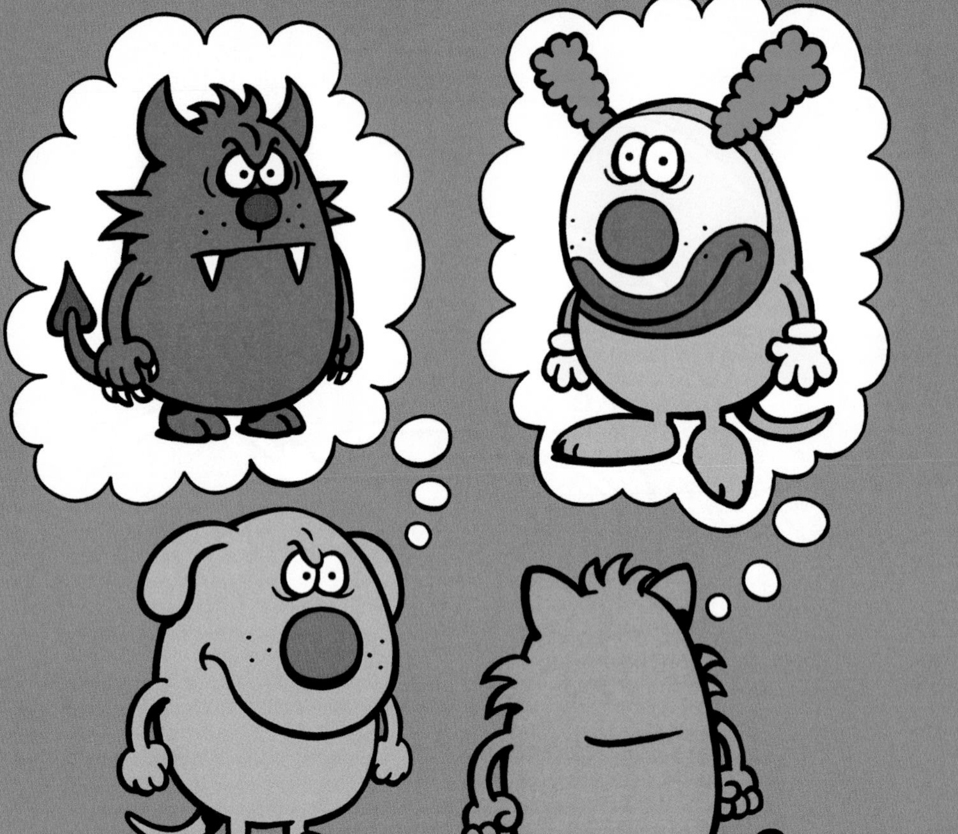

Pet hates

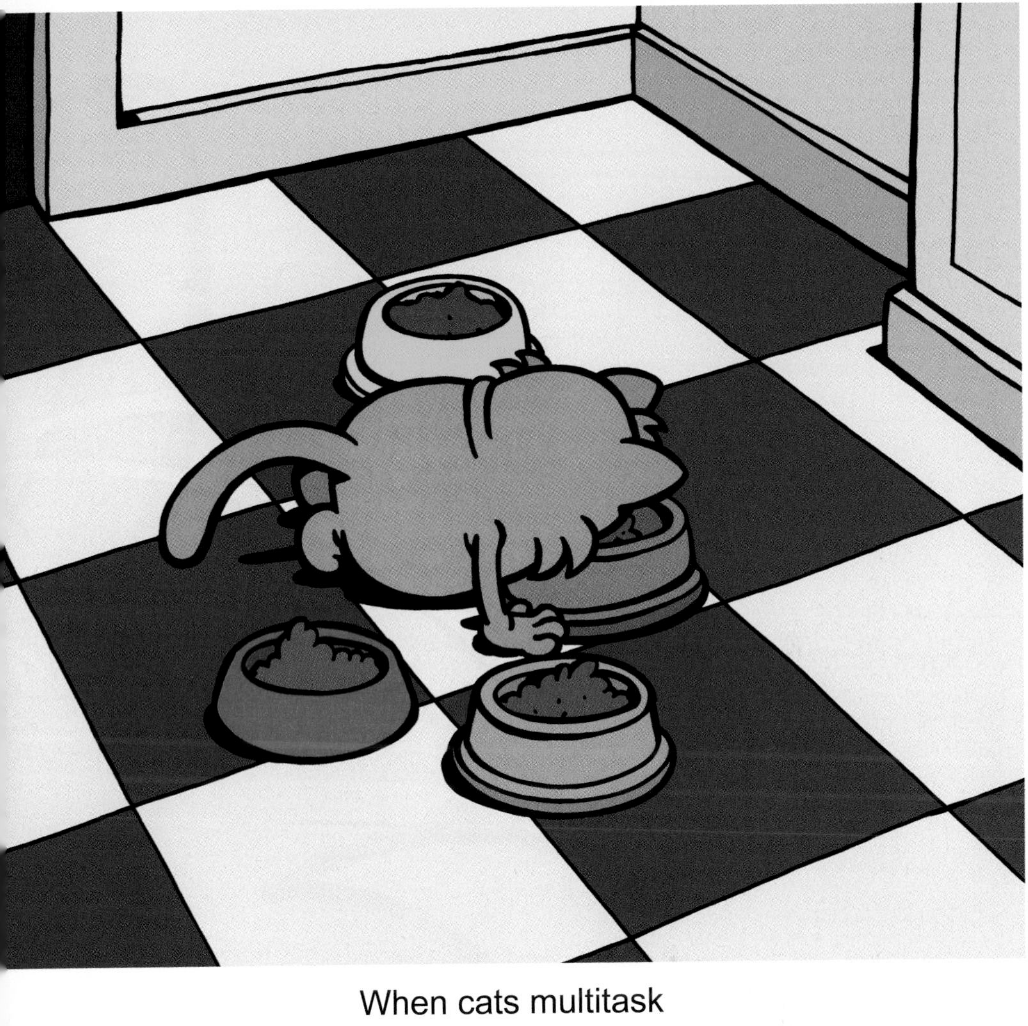

When cats multitask

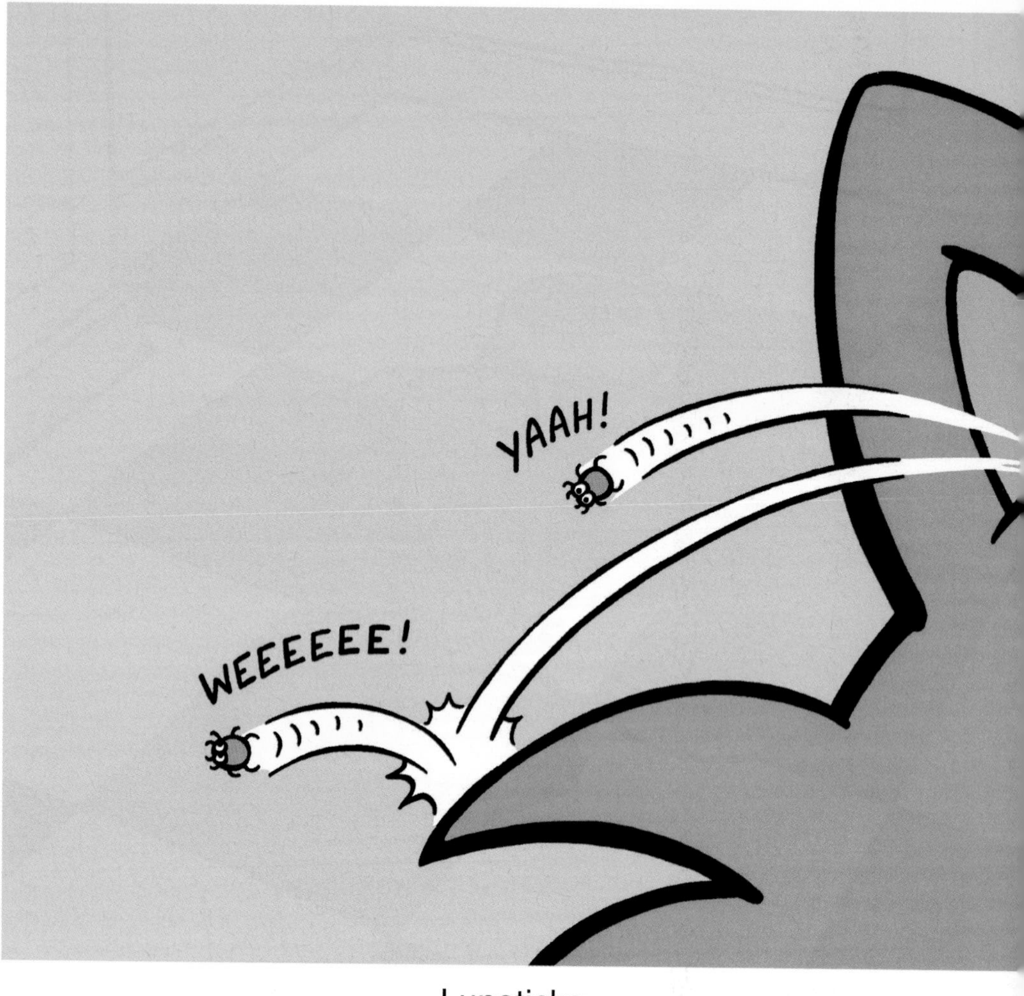
YAAH!
WEEEEEEE!

Lunaticks

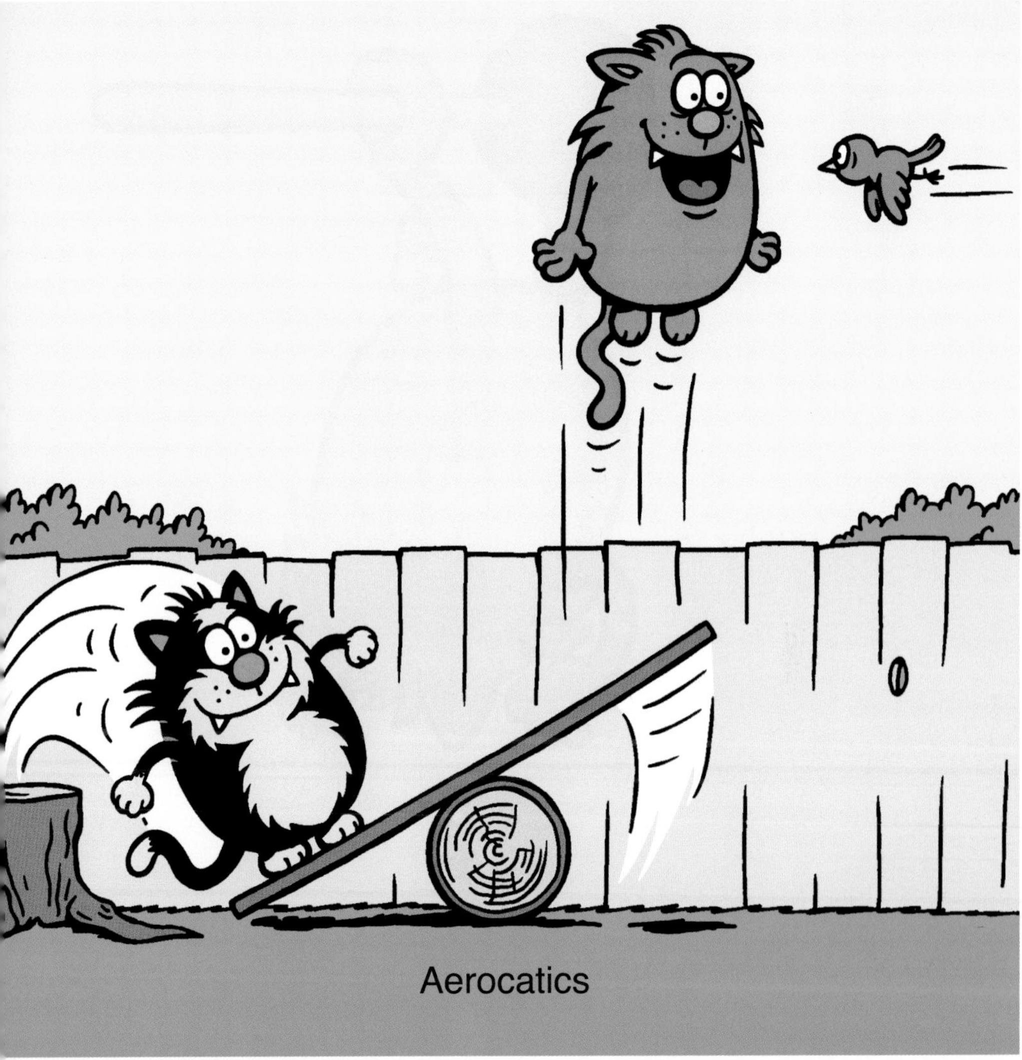

Aerocatics

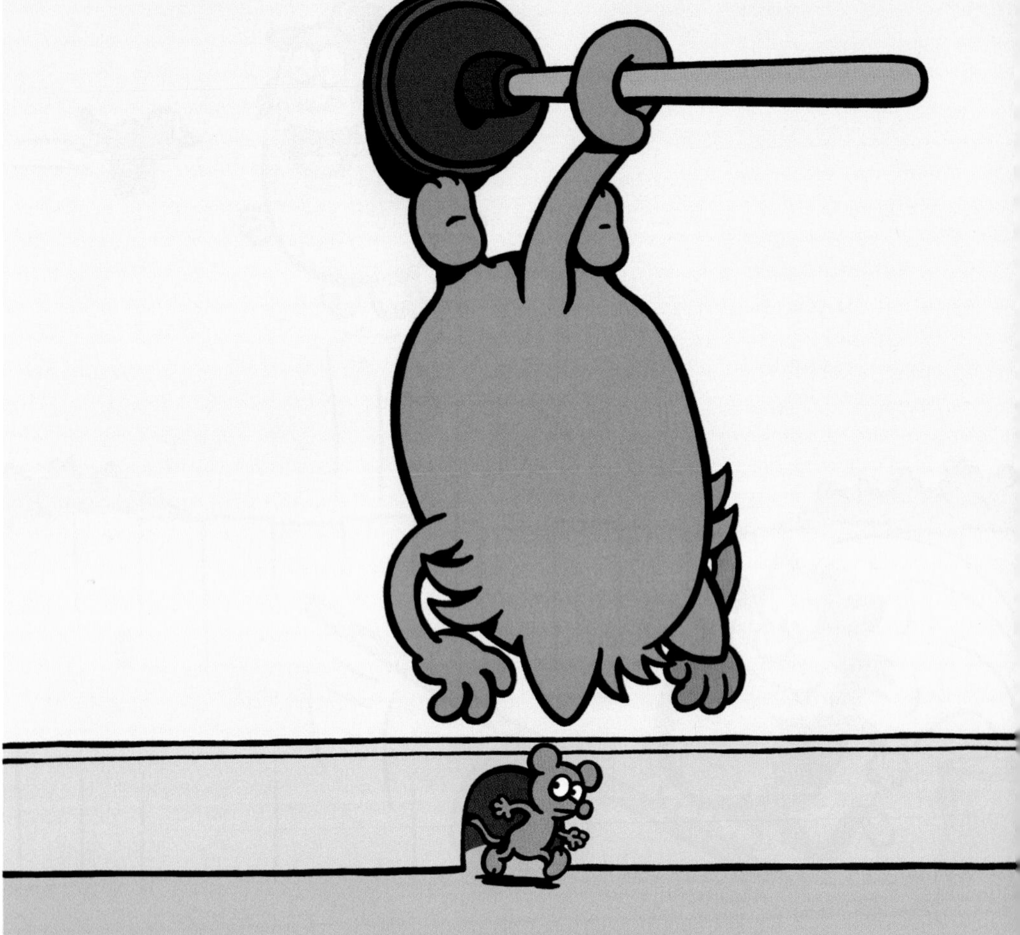

Suckering a mouse

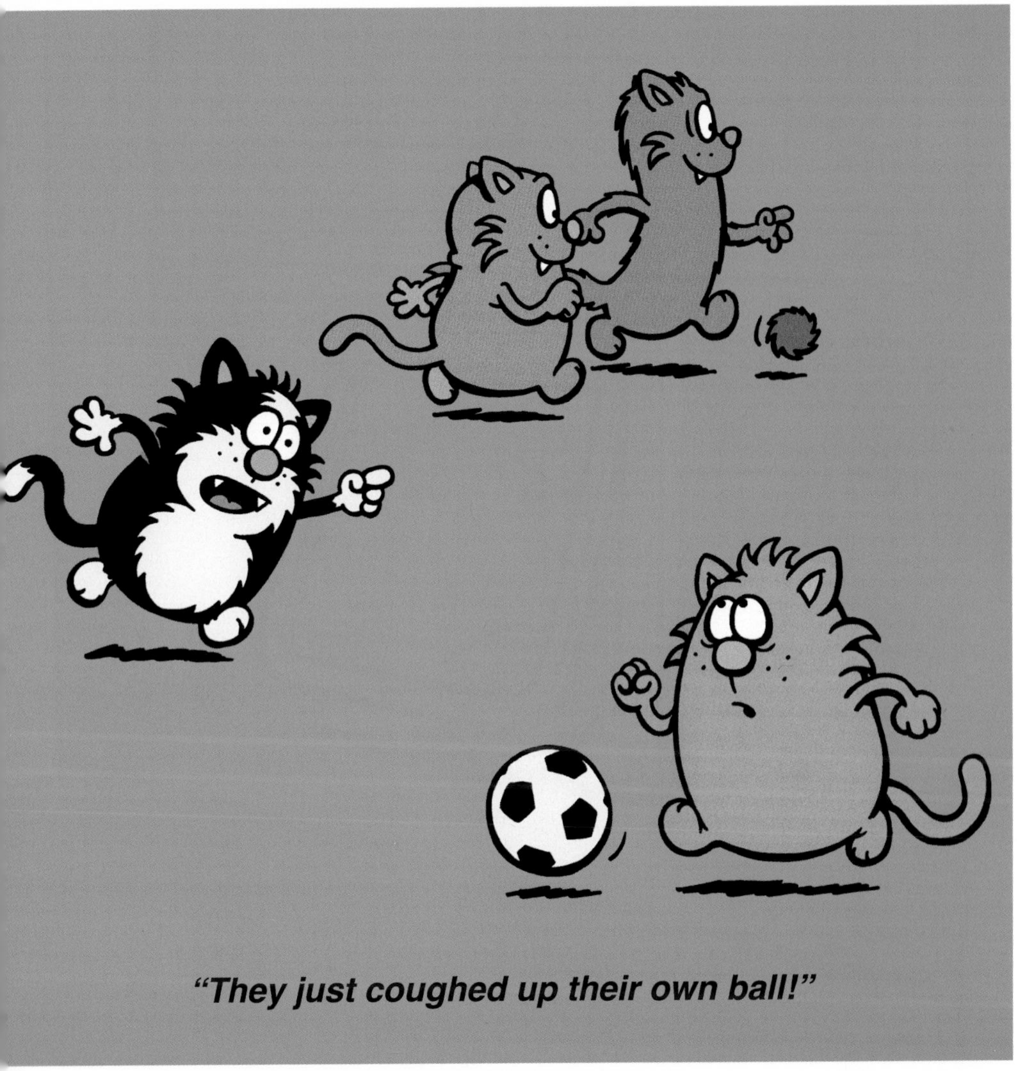

"They just coughed up their own ball!"

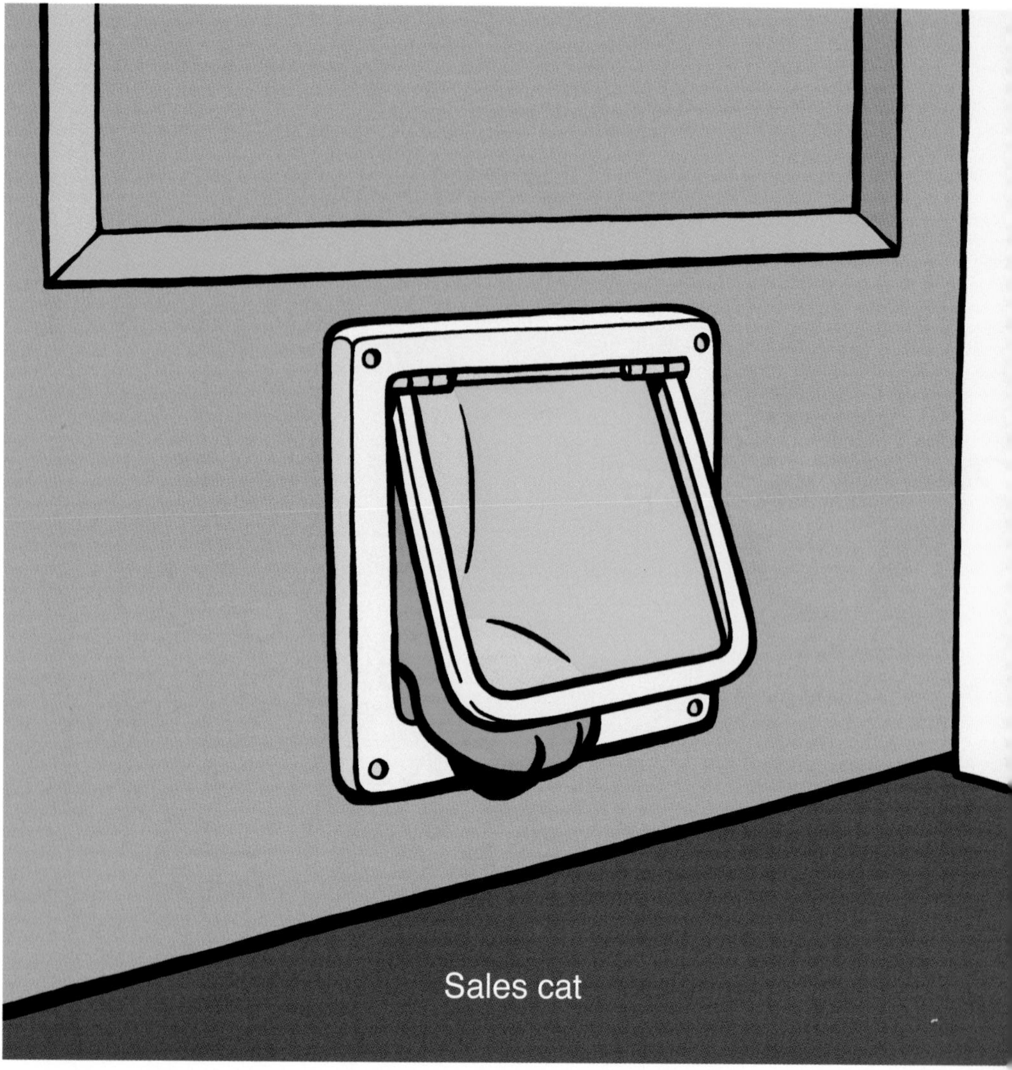

Sales cat

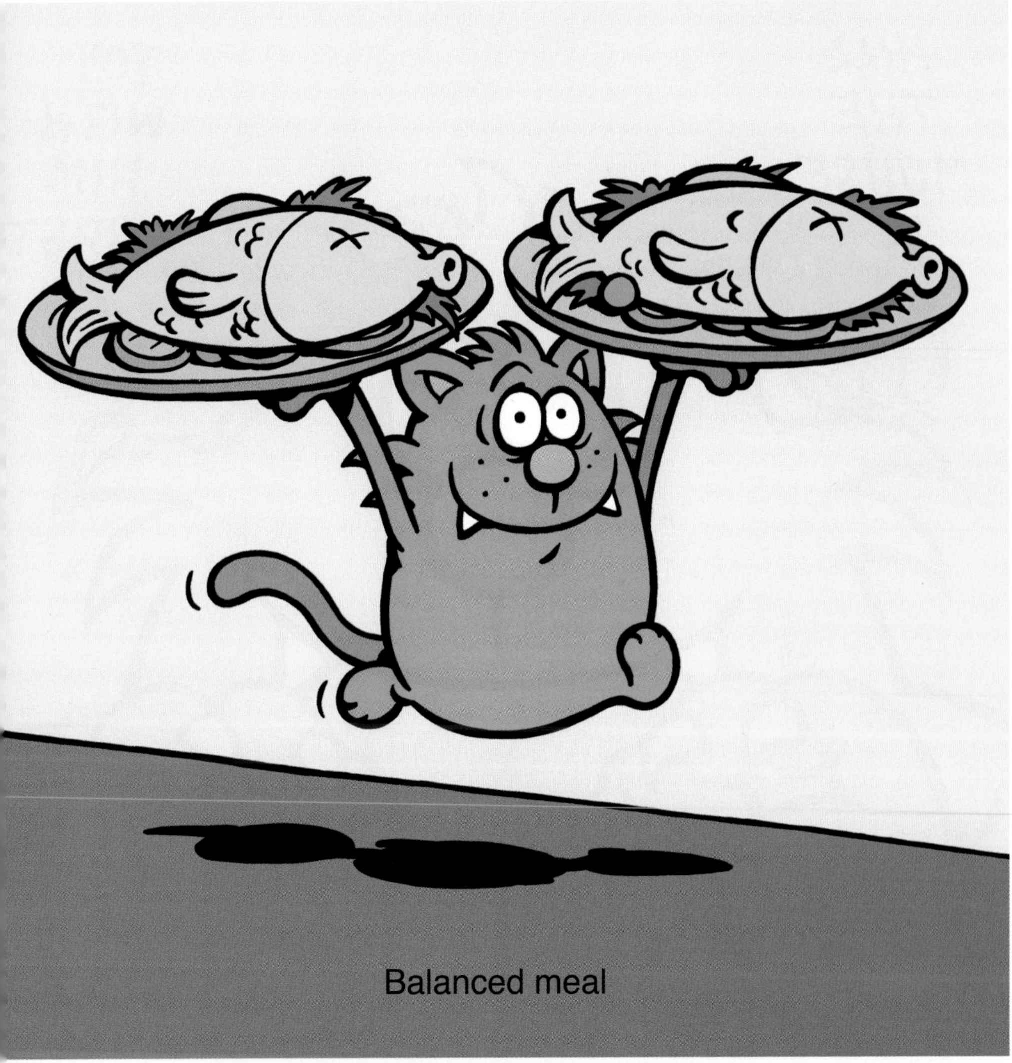

Balanced meal

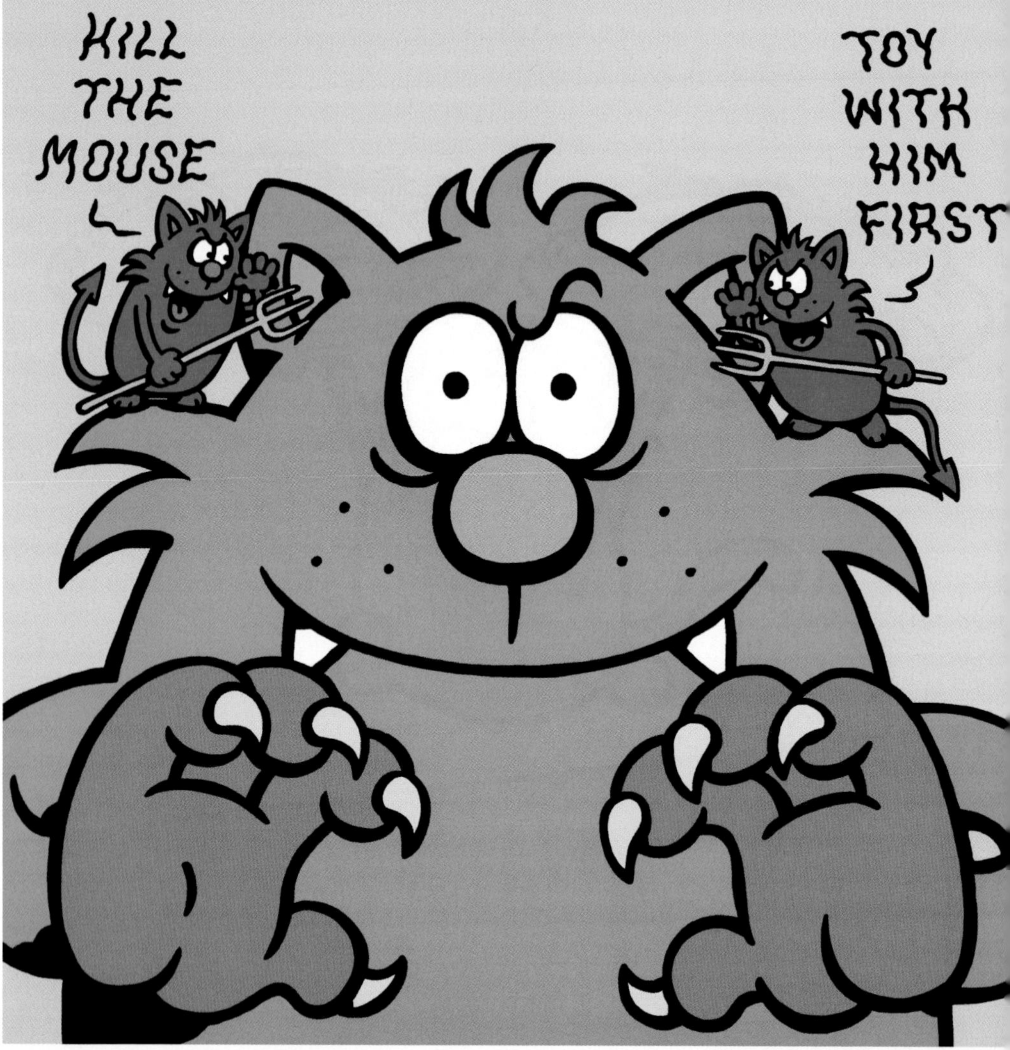
KILL THE MOUSE
TOY WITH HIM FIRST

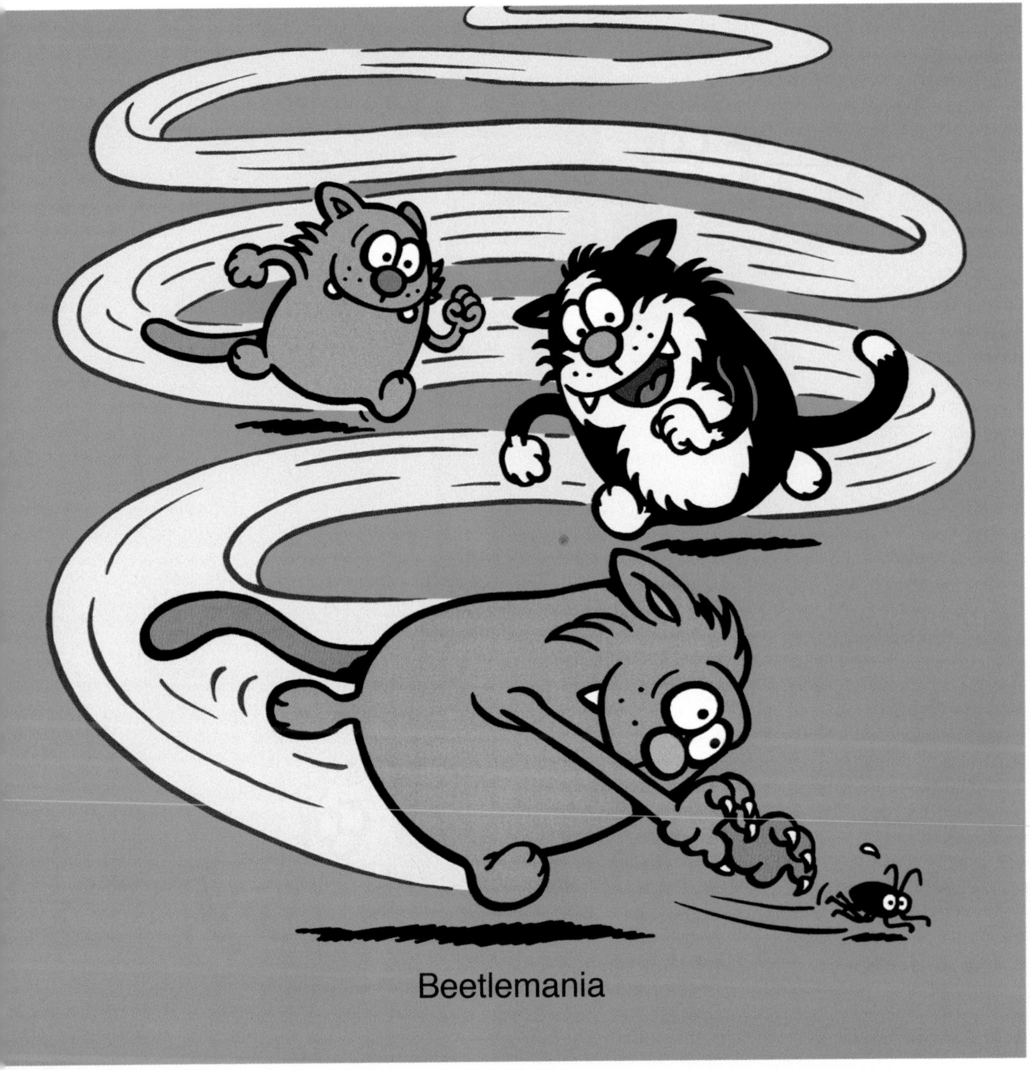

Beetlemania

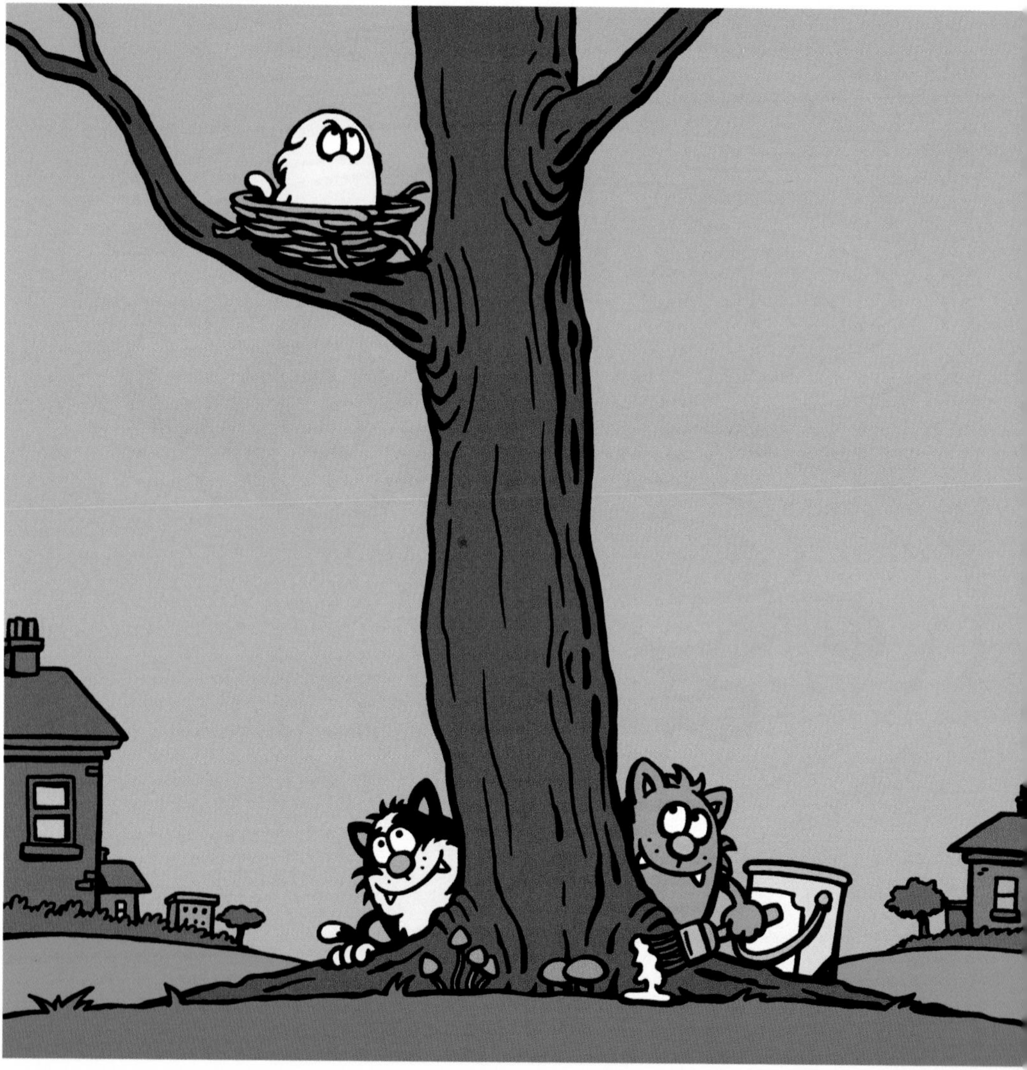

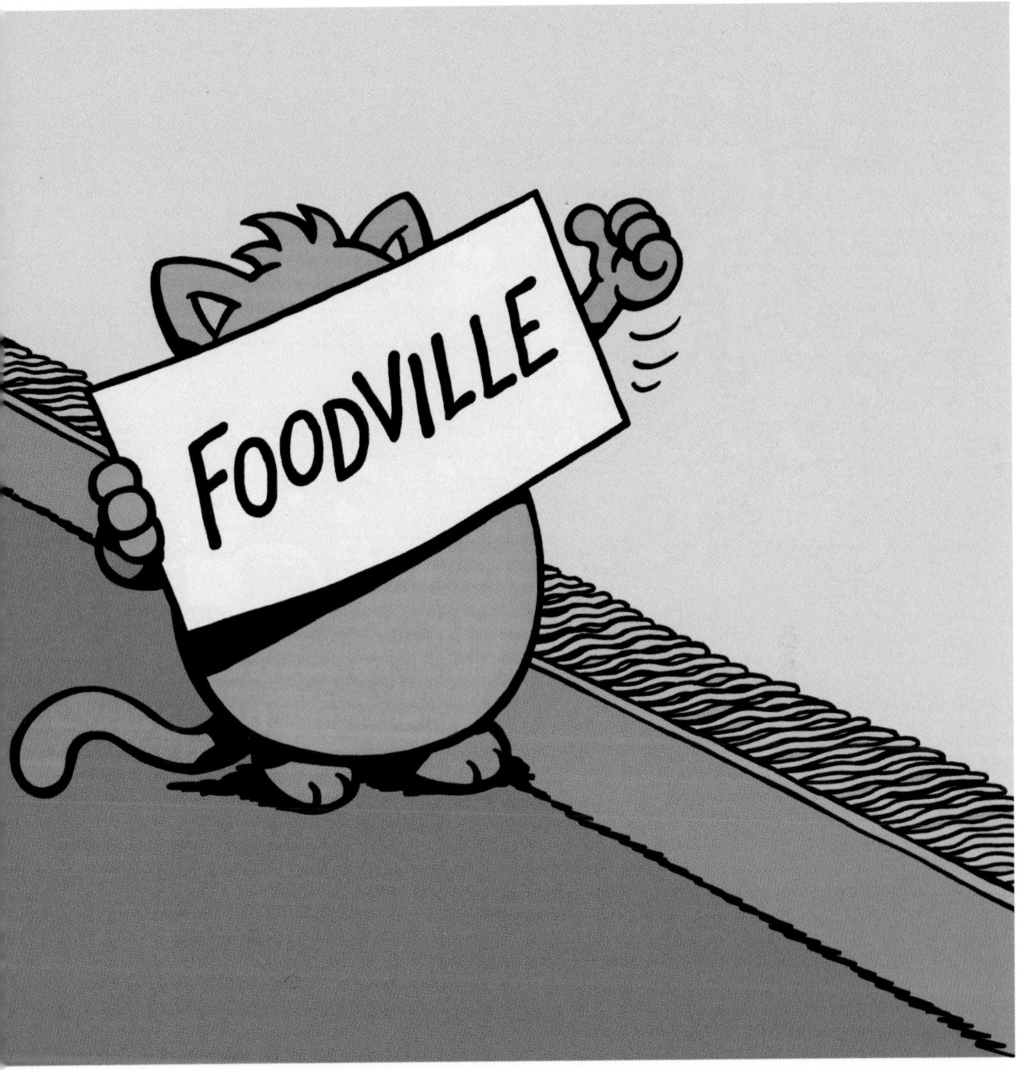
FOODVILLE

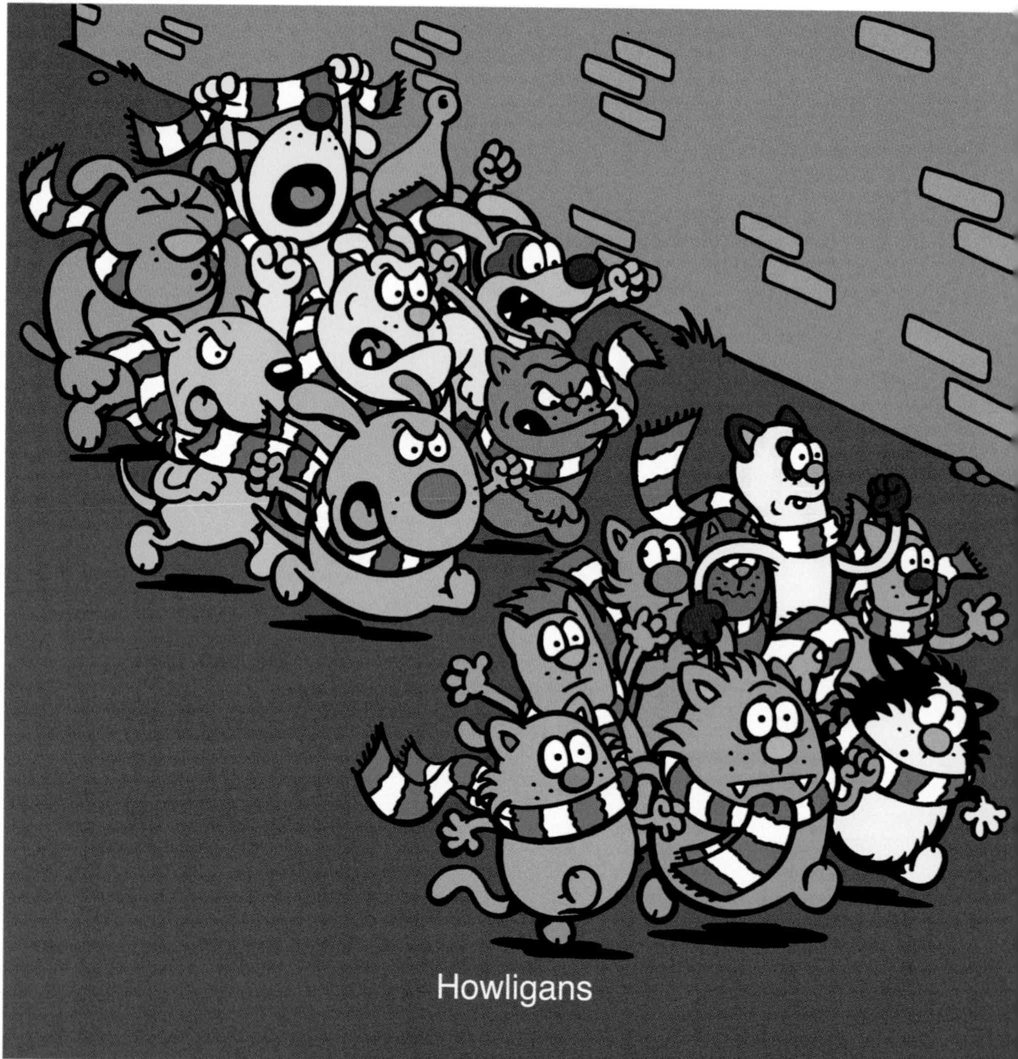

Howligans

MOL

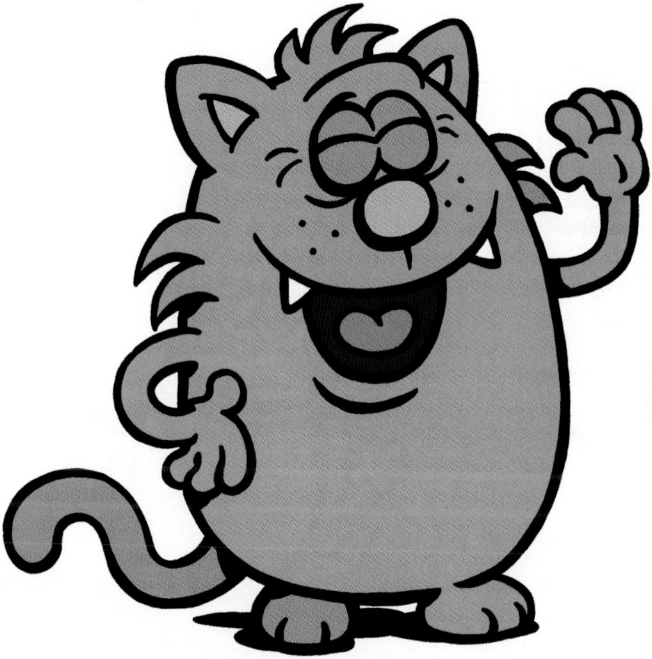

Meow out loud

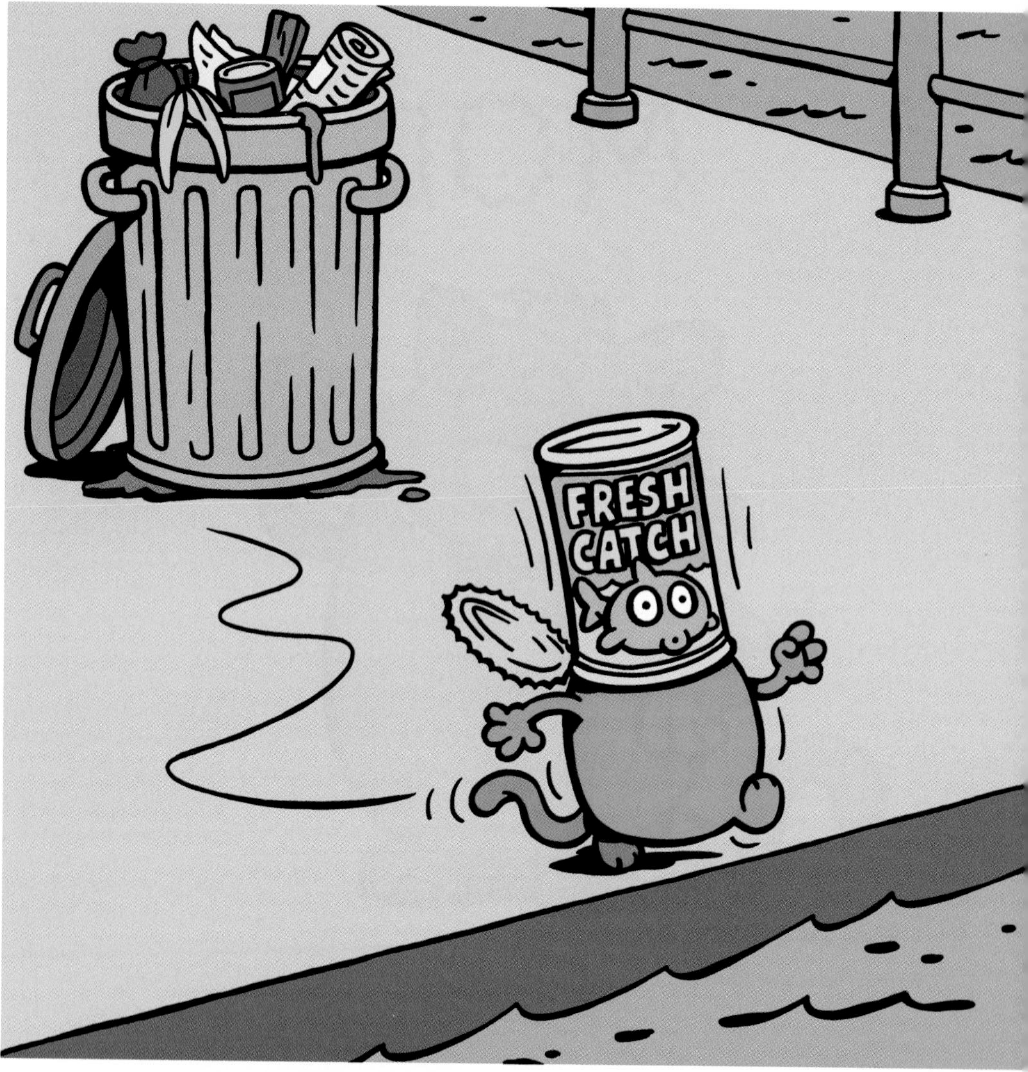
FRESH
CATCH

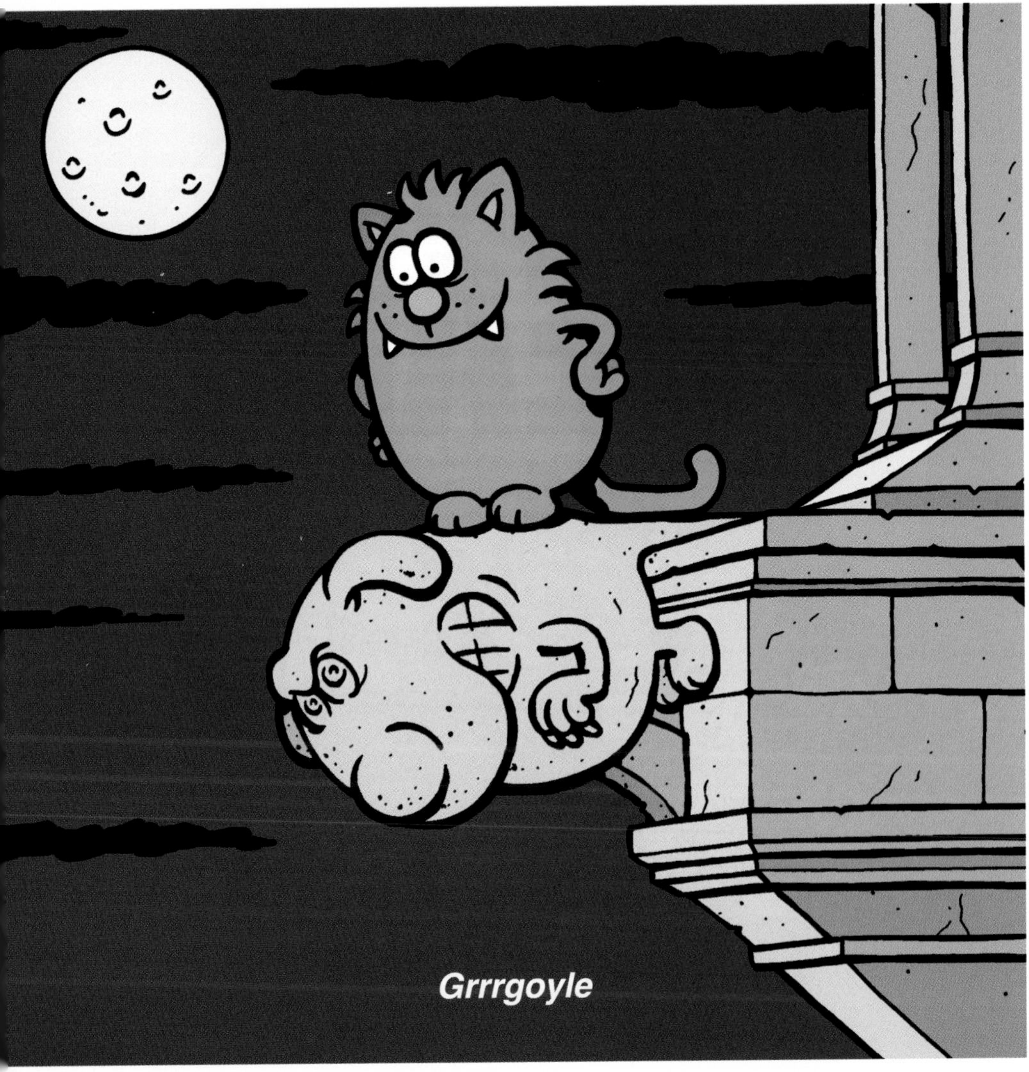
Grrrgoyle

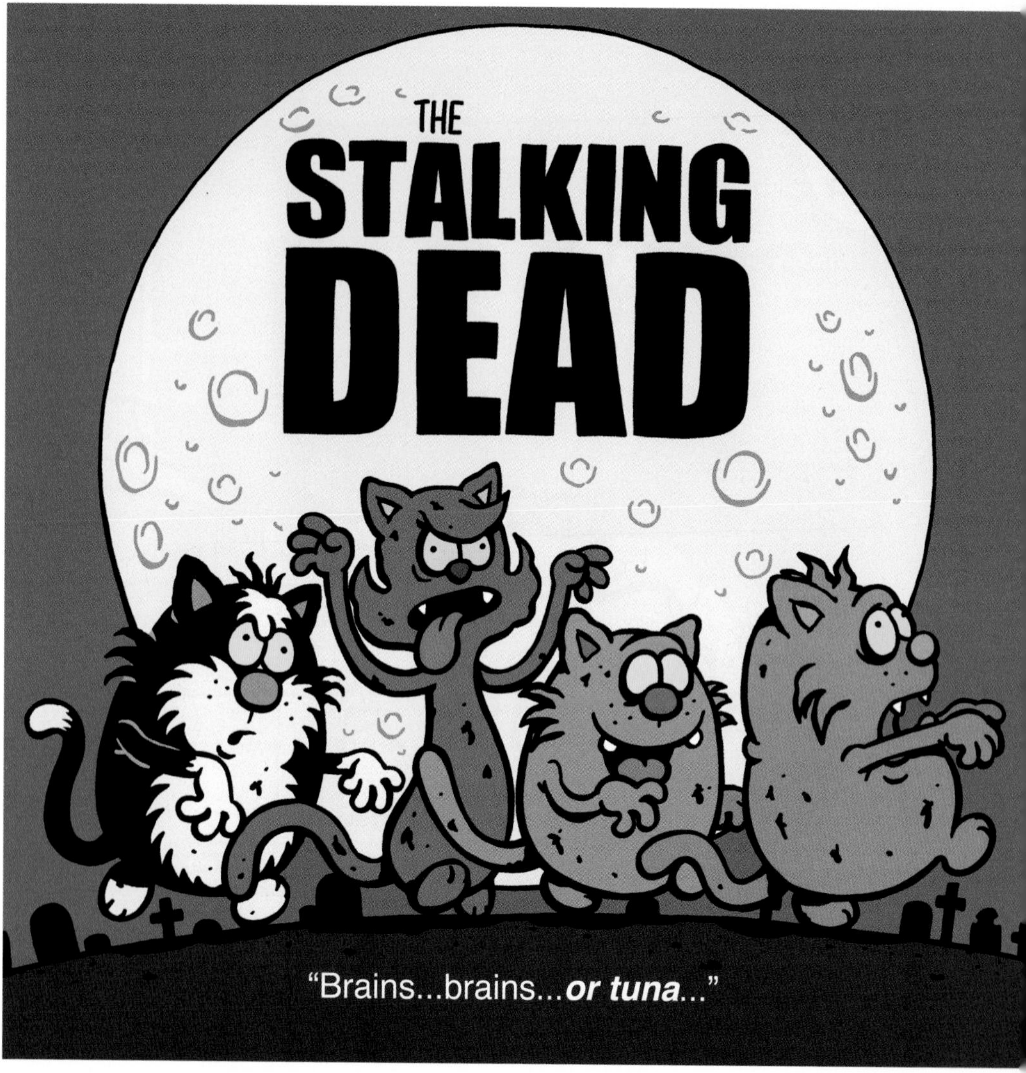
THE
STALKING
DEAD

"Brains...brains...***or tuna***..."

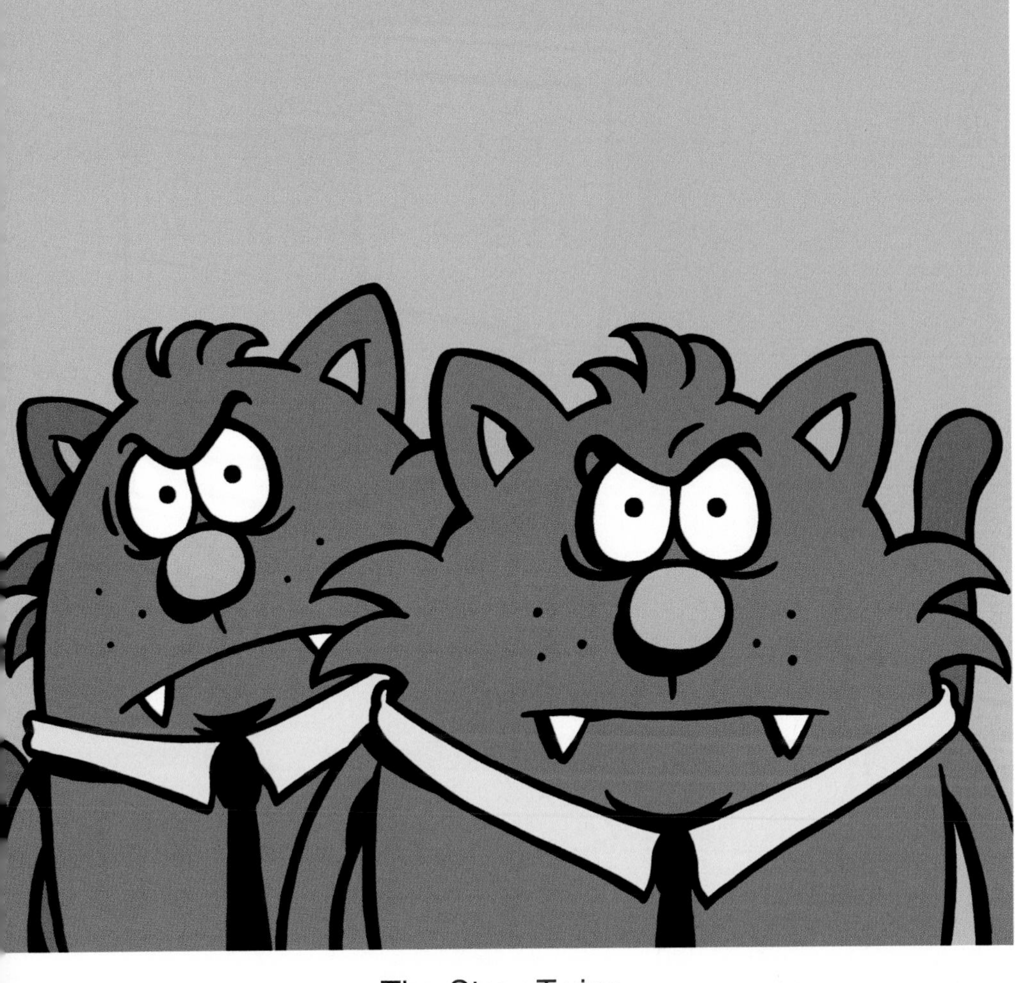

The Stray Twins

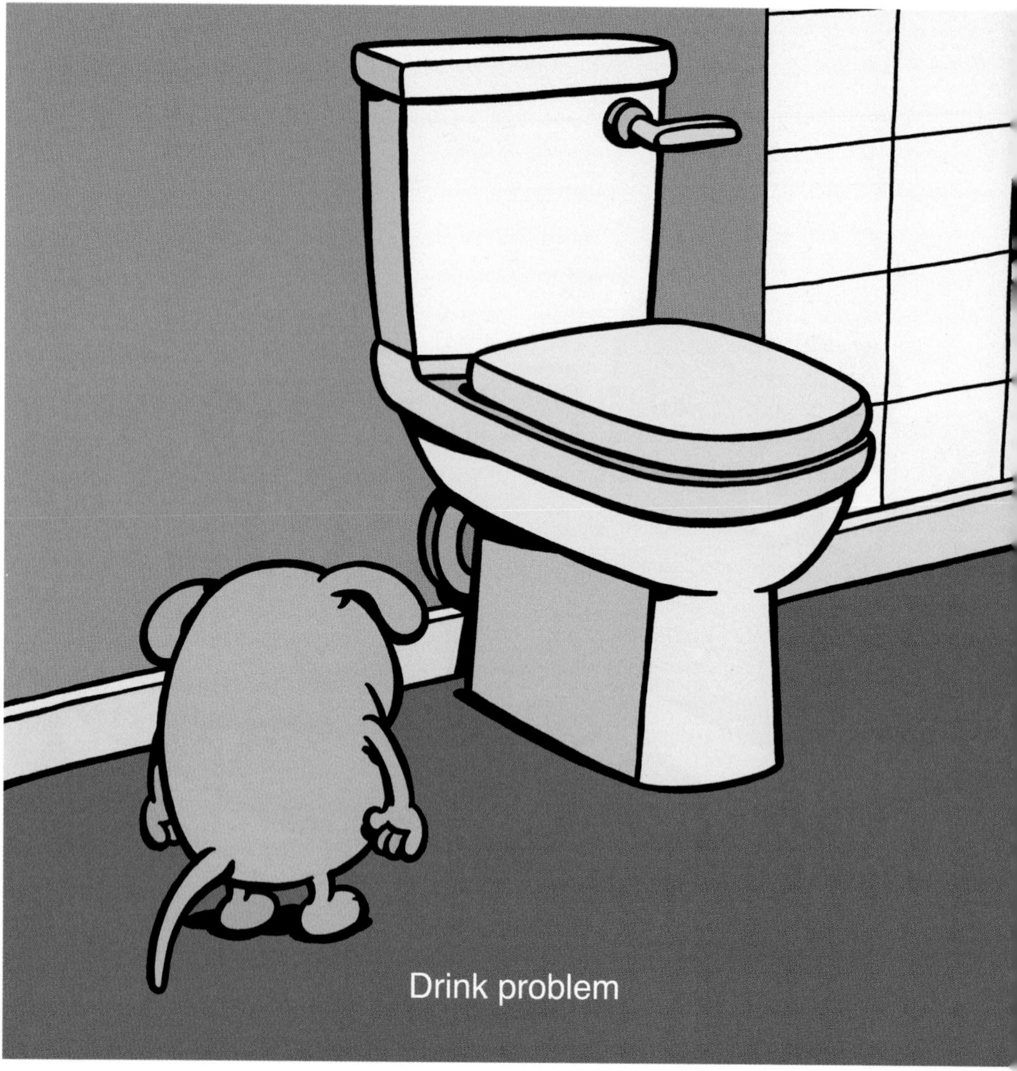
Drink problem

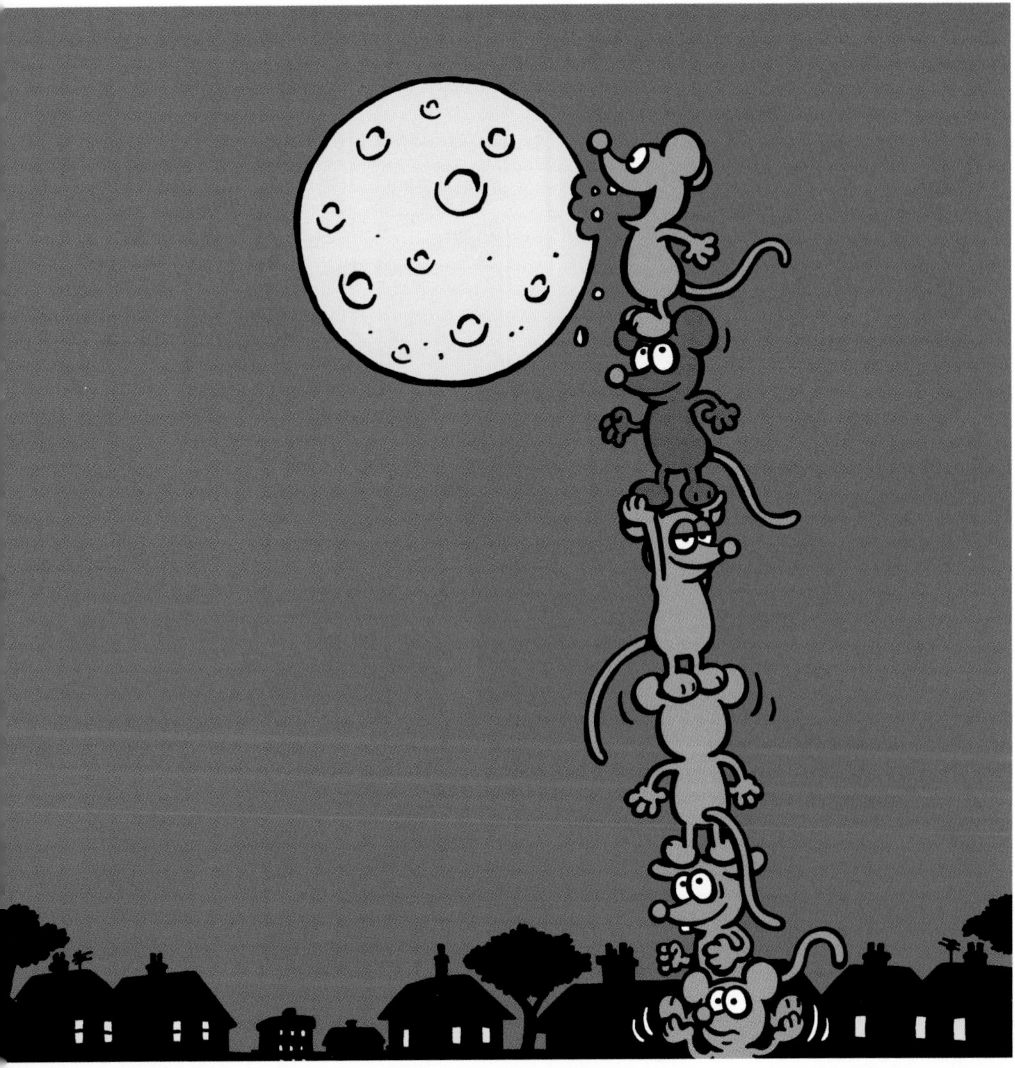

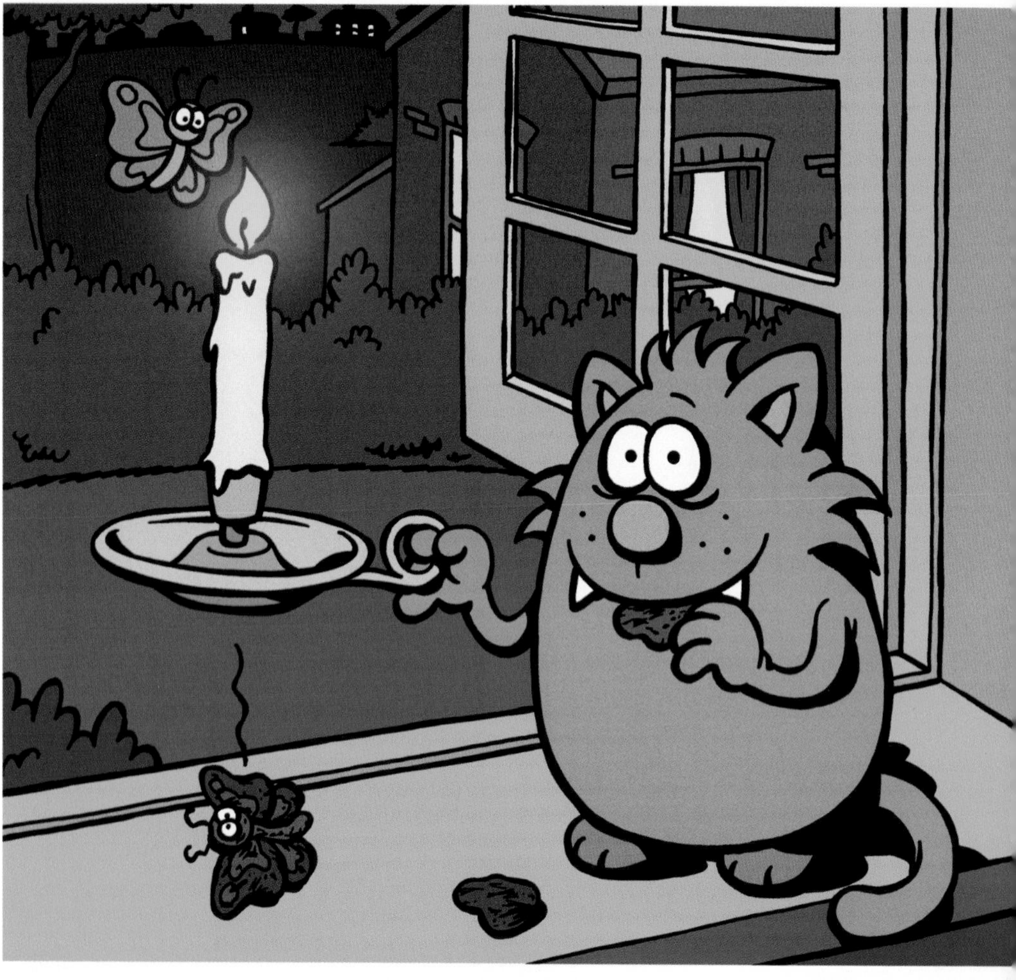

Hot wings

PURRATE

" Avast, ye scurvy sea-dog!"

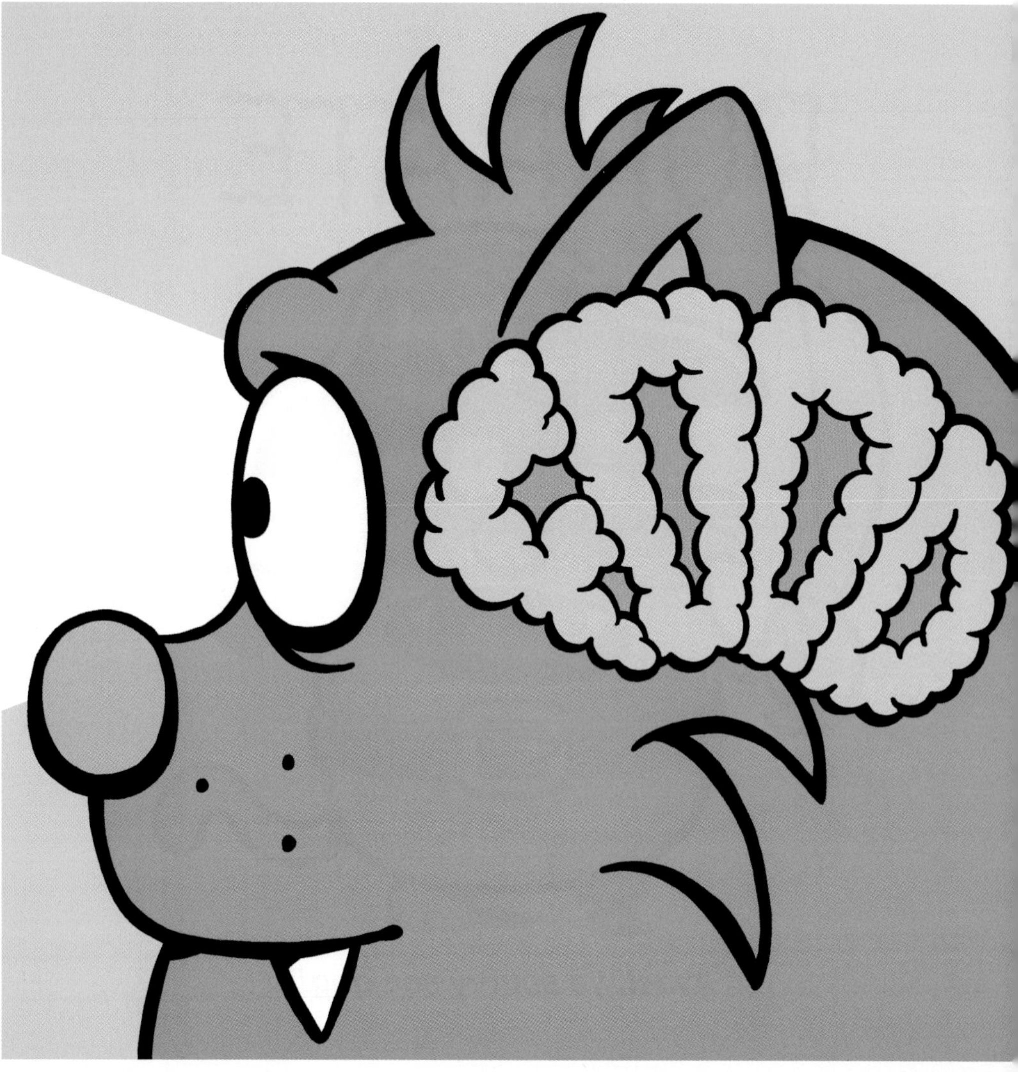

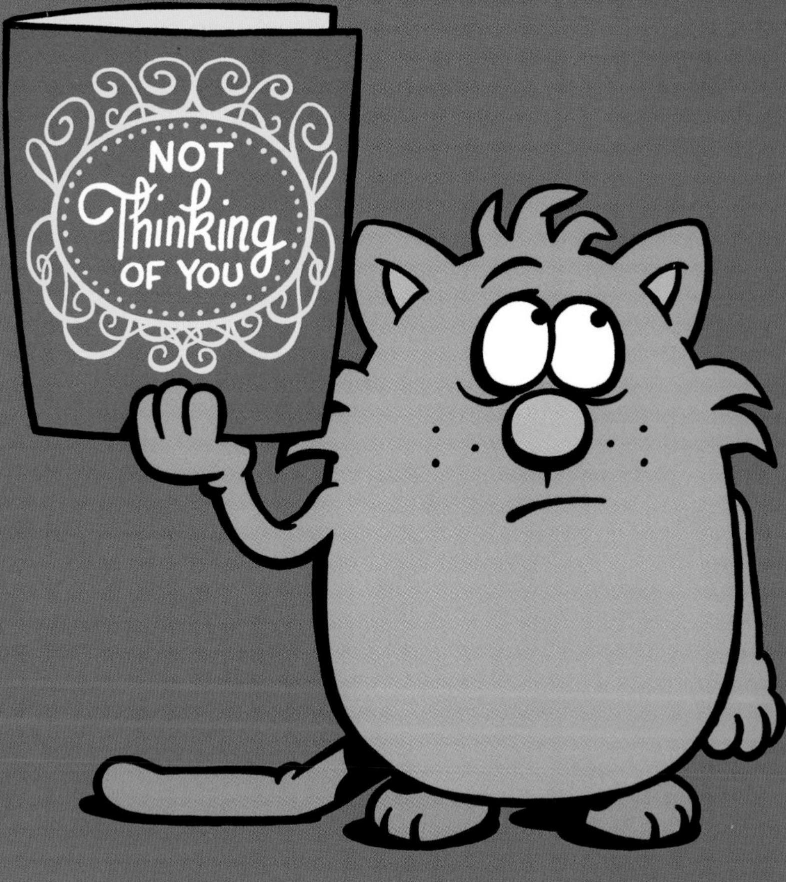
NOT
Thinking
OF YOU

If cats gave cards

How cats use Twitter...

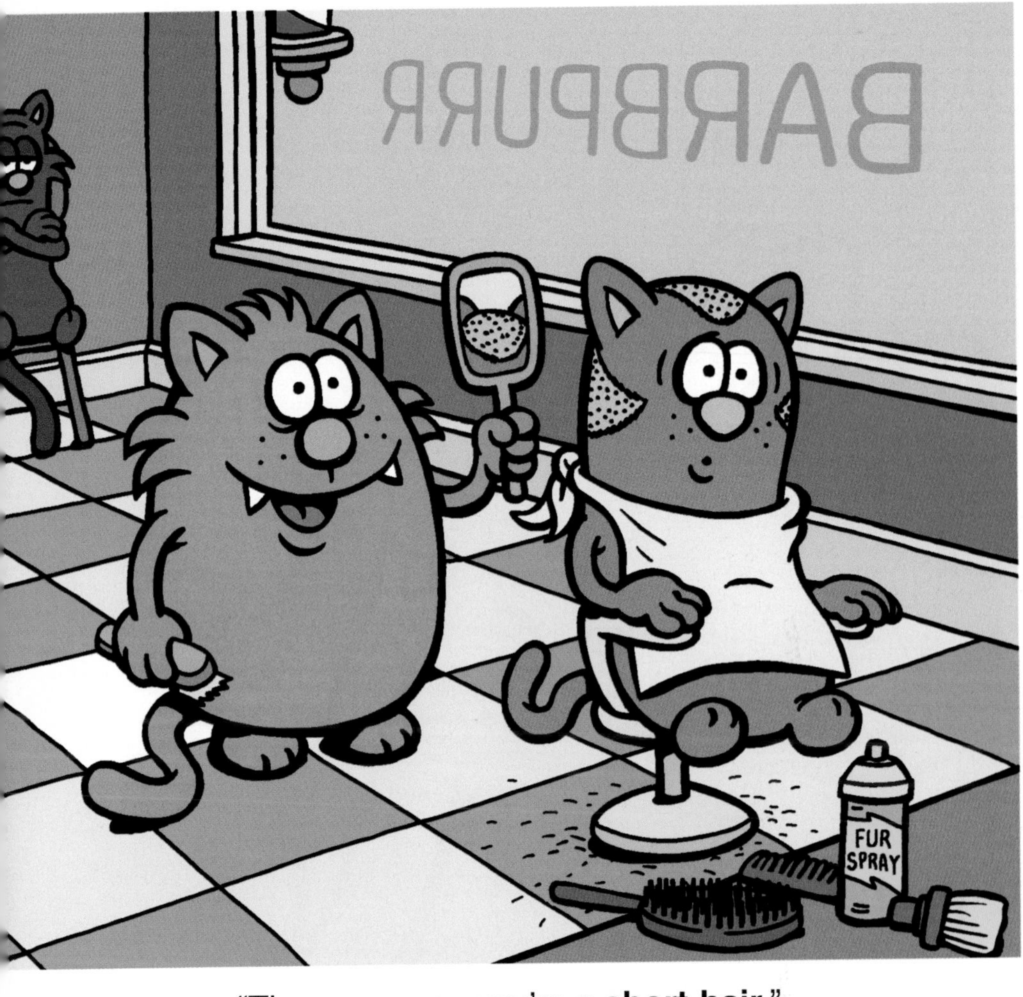
BARBPURR
FUR SPRAY

"There you go...you're a **short-hair**."

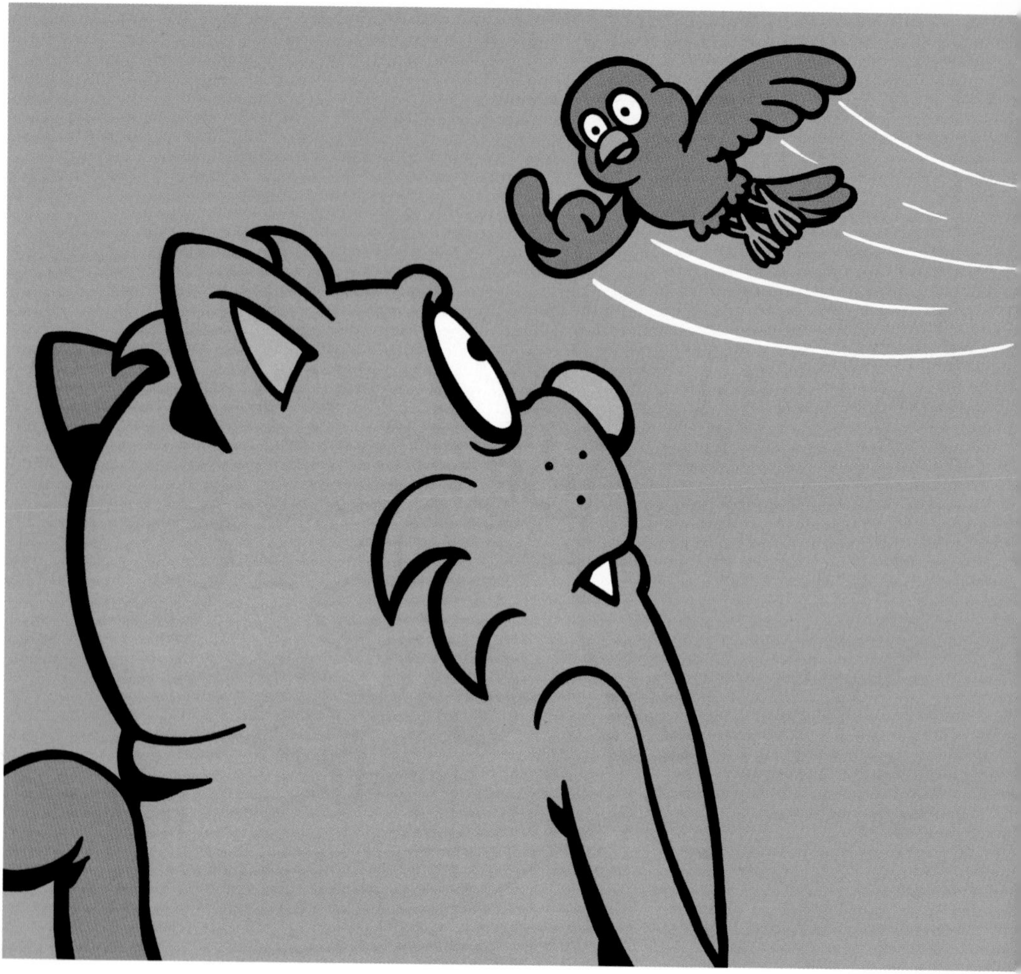

Getting the bird

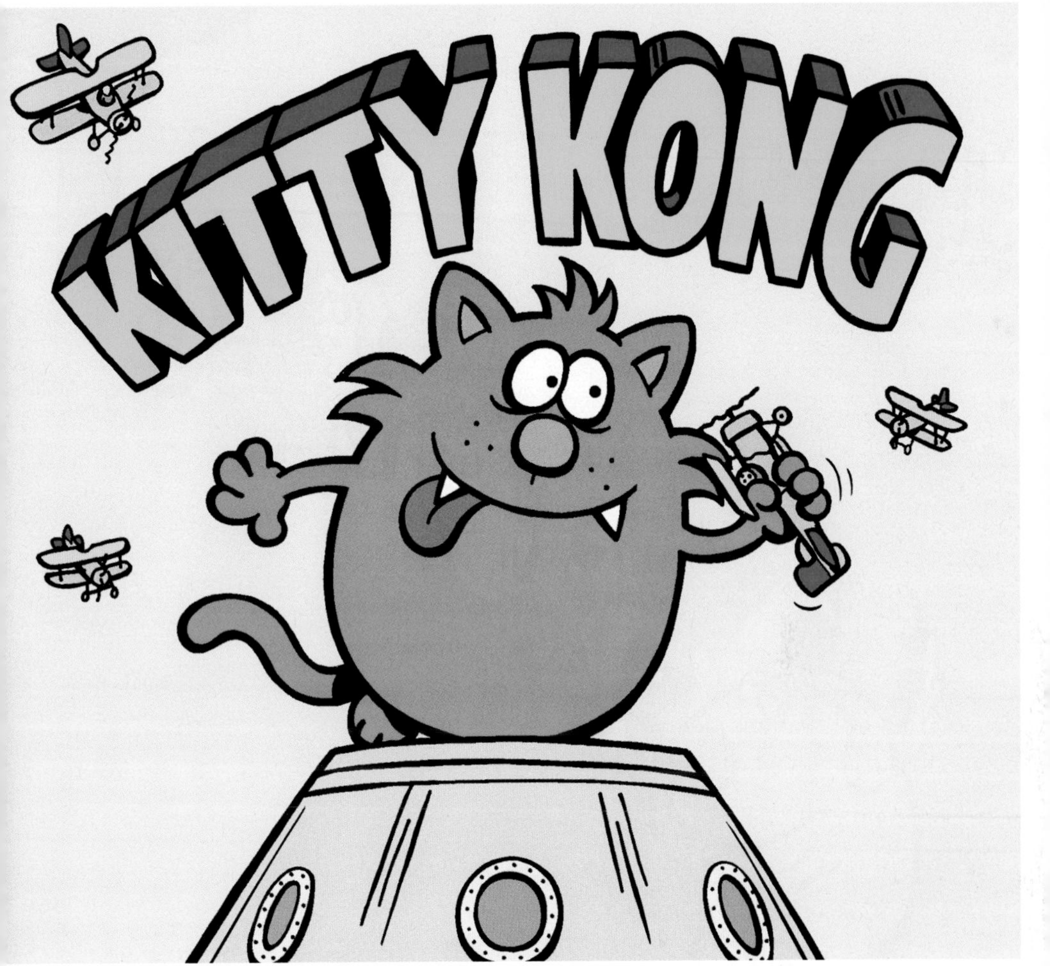
KITTY KONG

Mmm...Crunchy birdies."

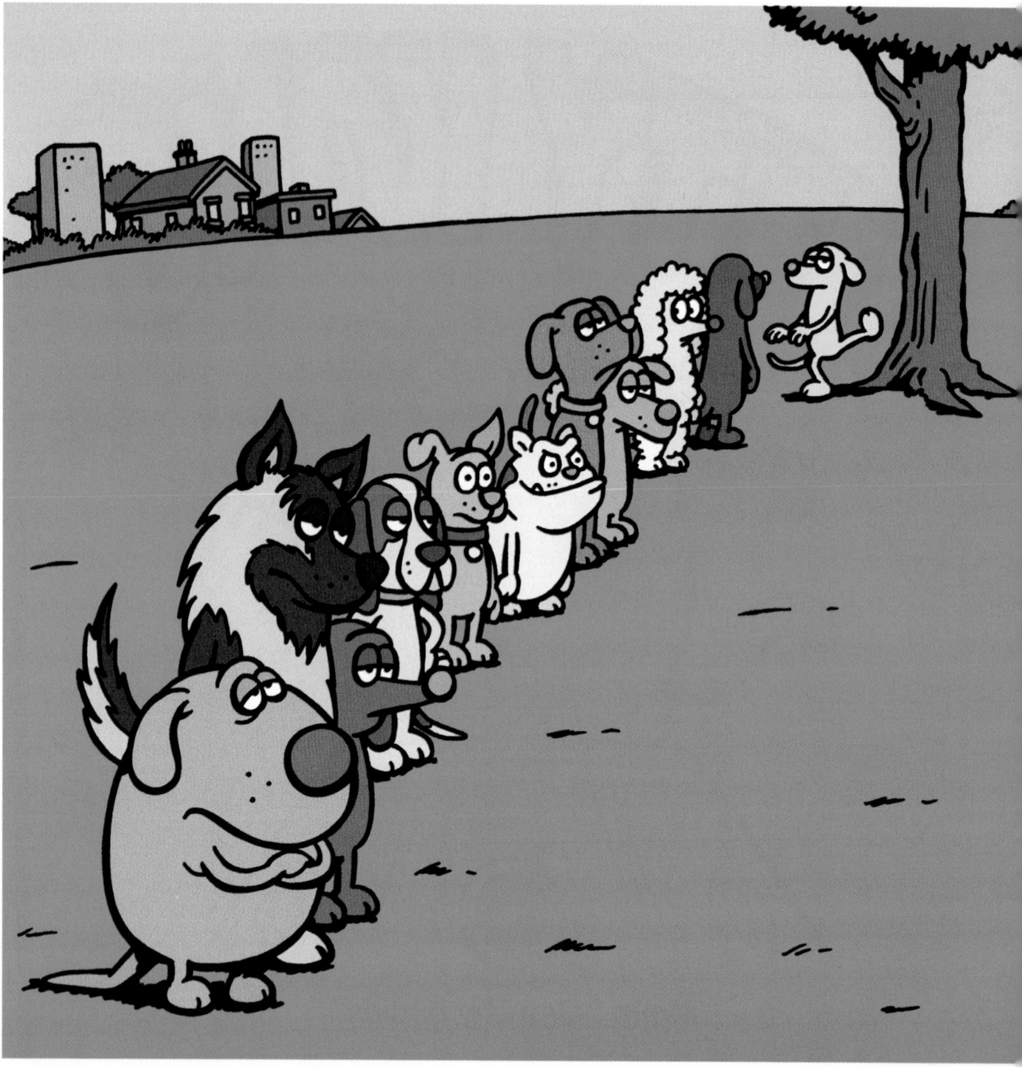

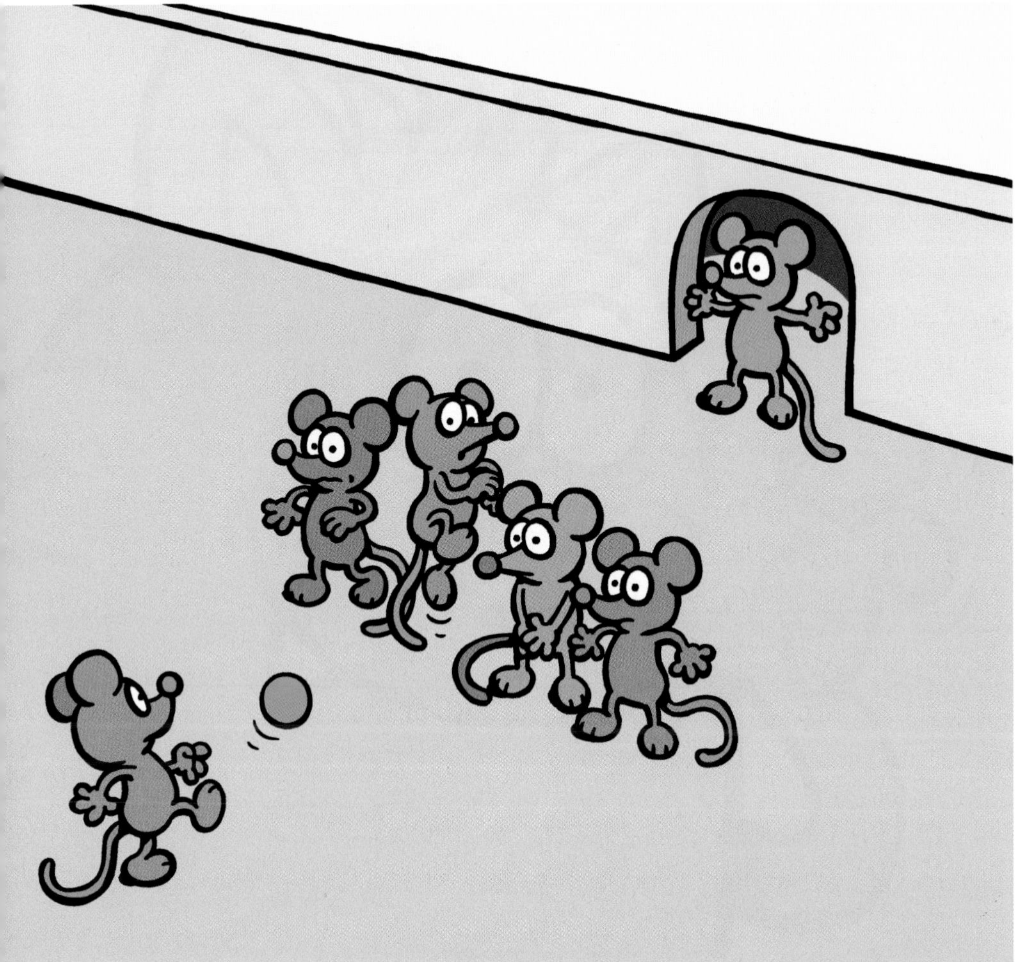

Pea kick

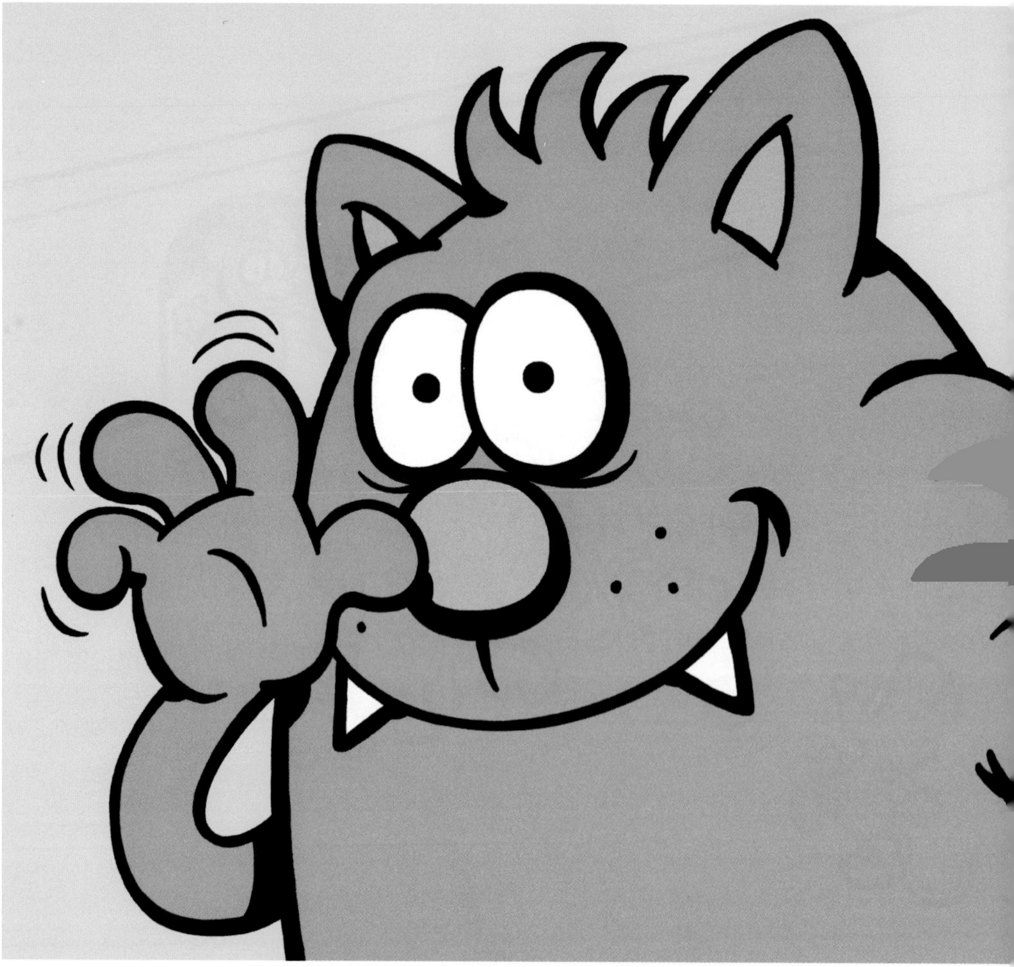

Paw response to training

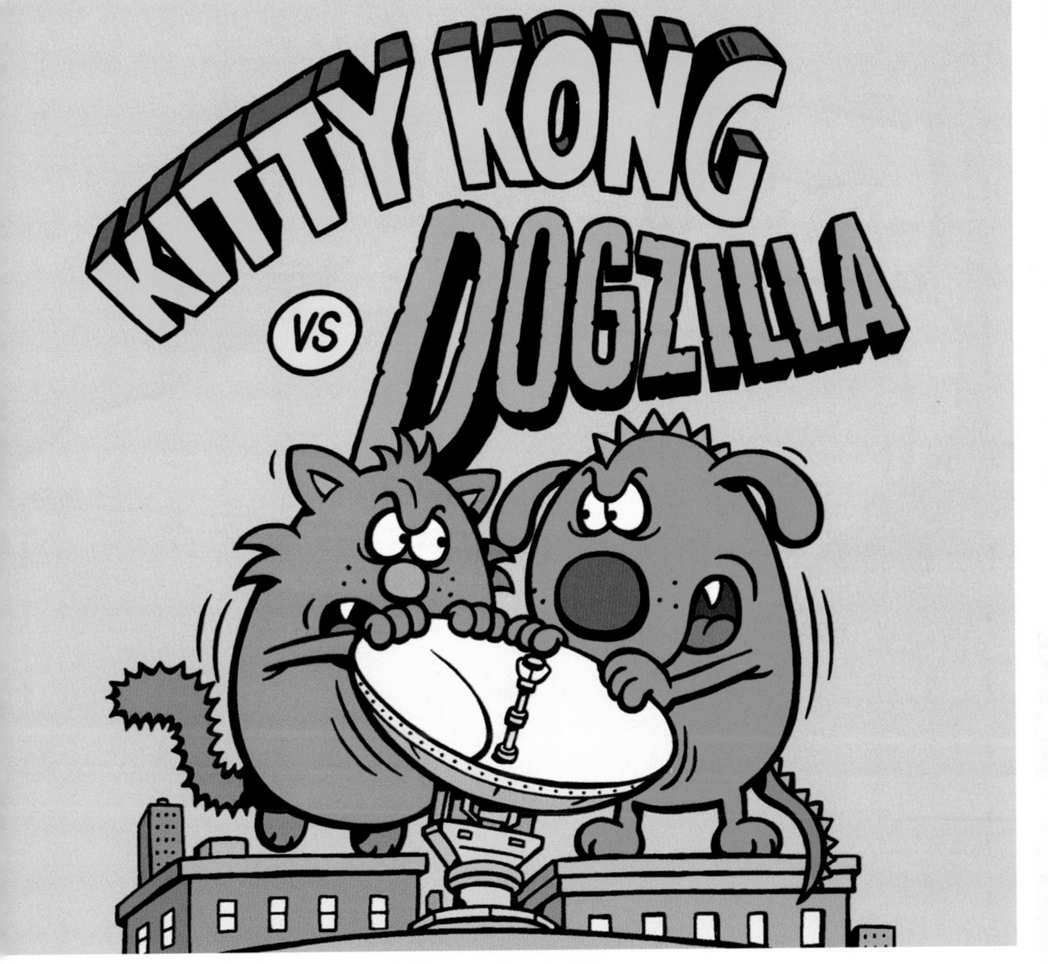
KITTY KONG
VS
DOGZILLA

"My dish!!!"

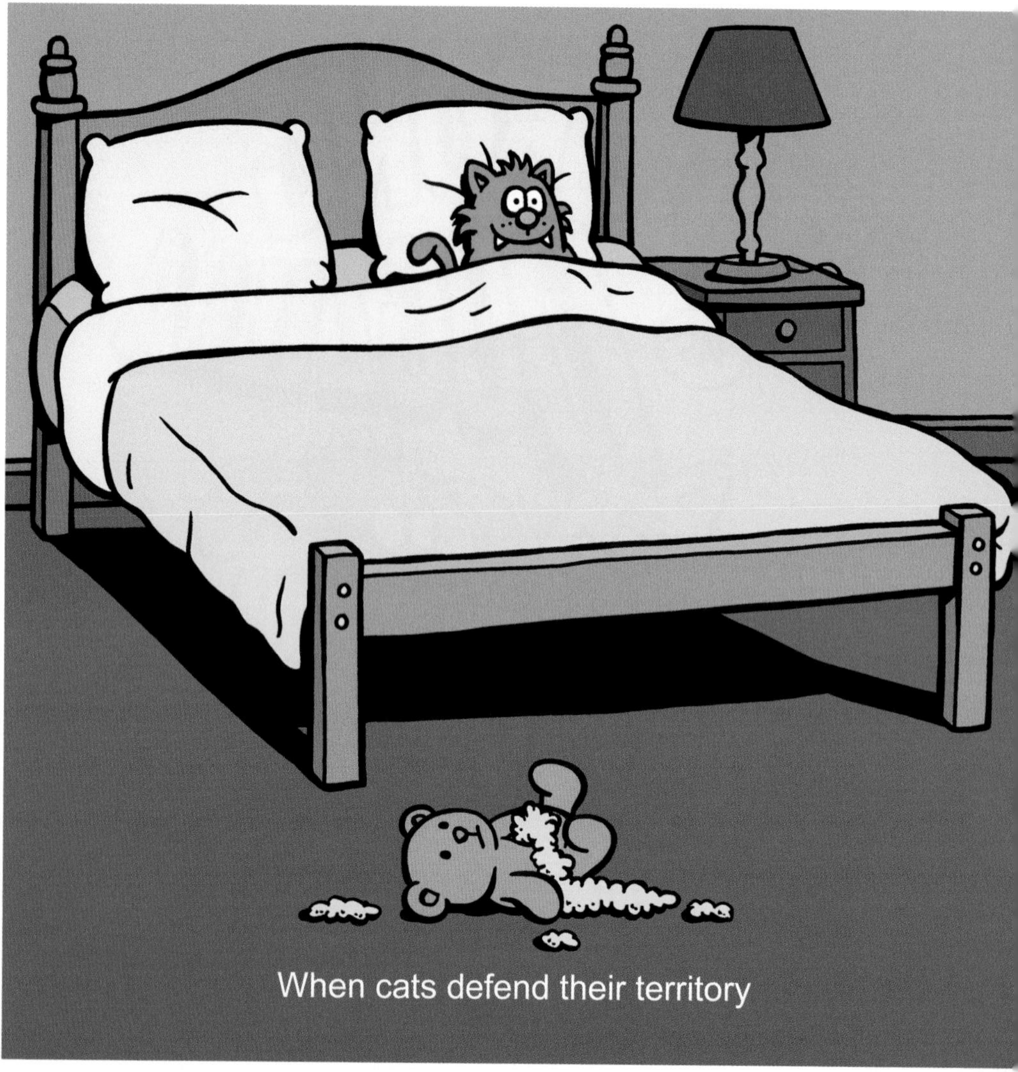

When cats defend their territory

Apusstrophe

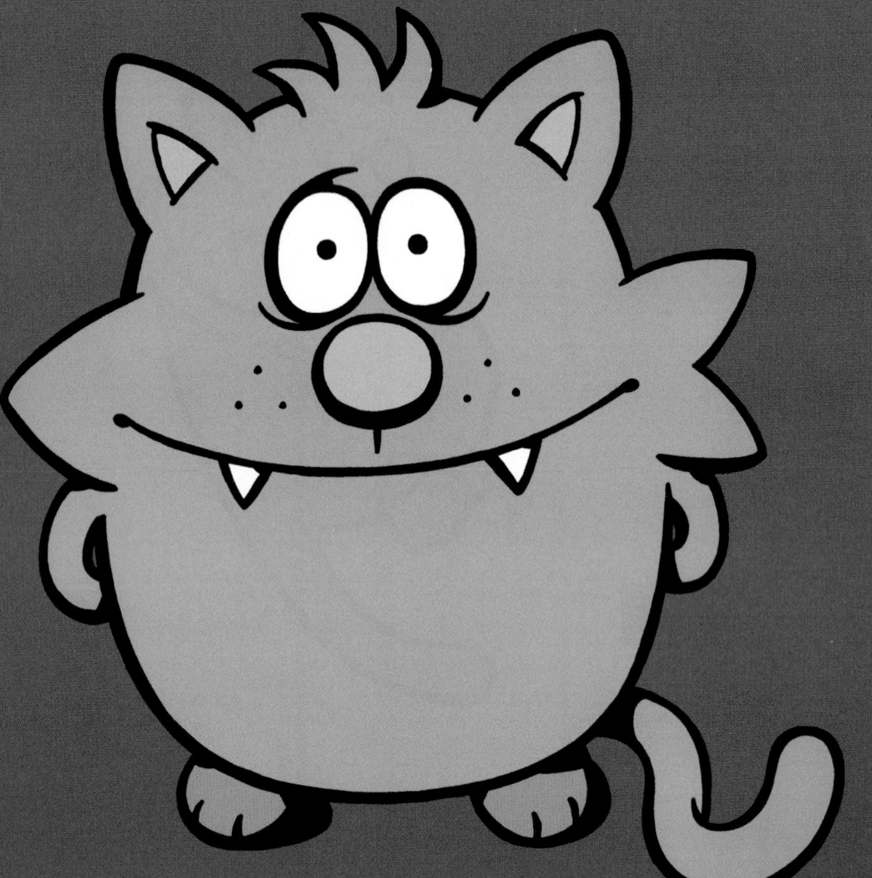

"What fish?"

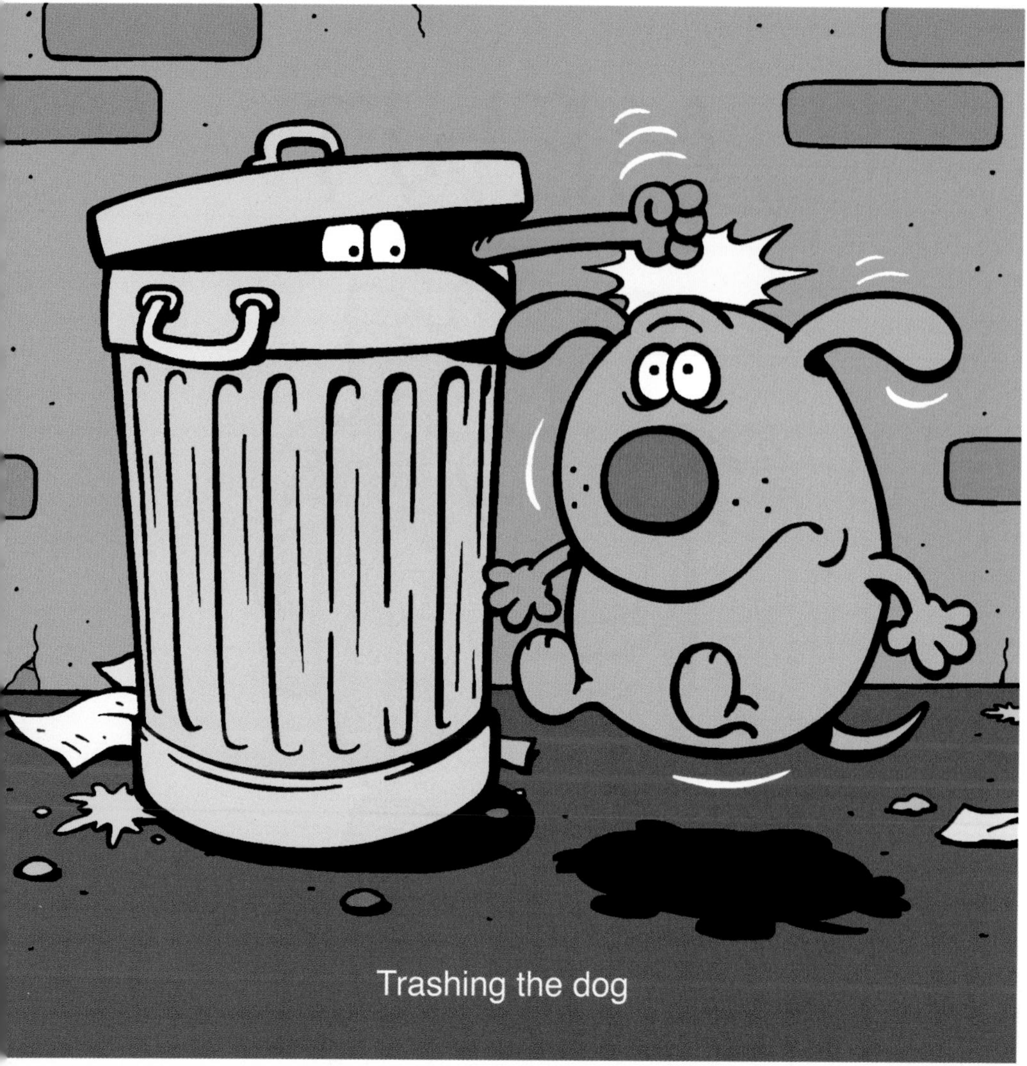

Trashing the dog

MEWT

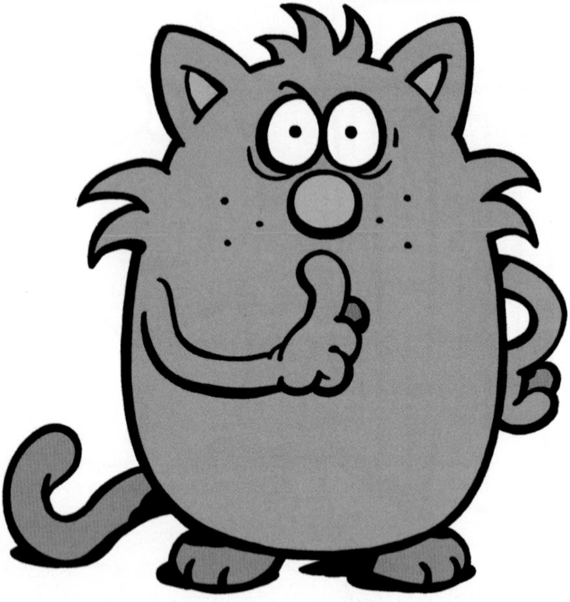

"Silence, human."

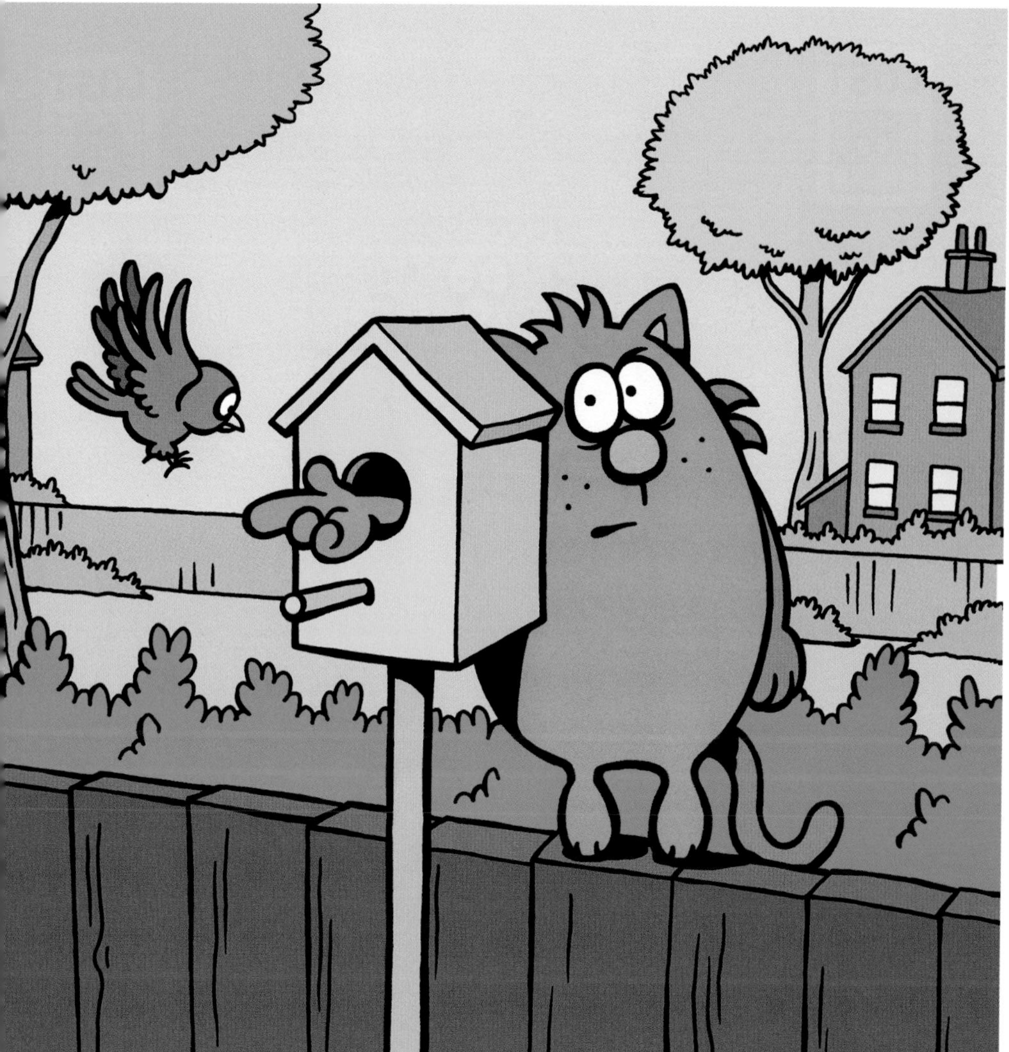

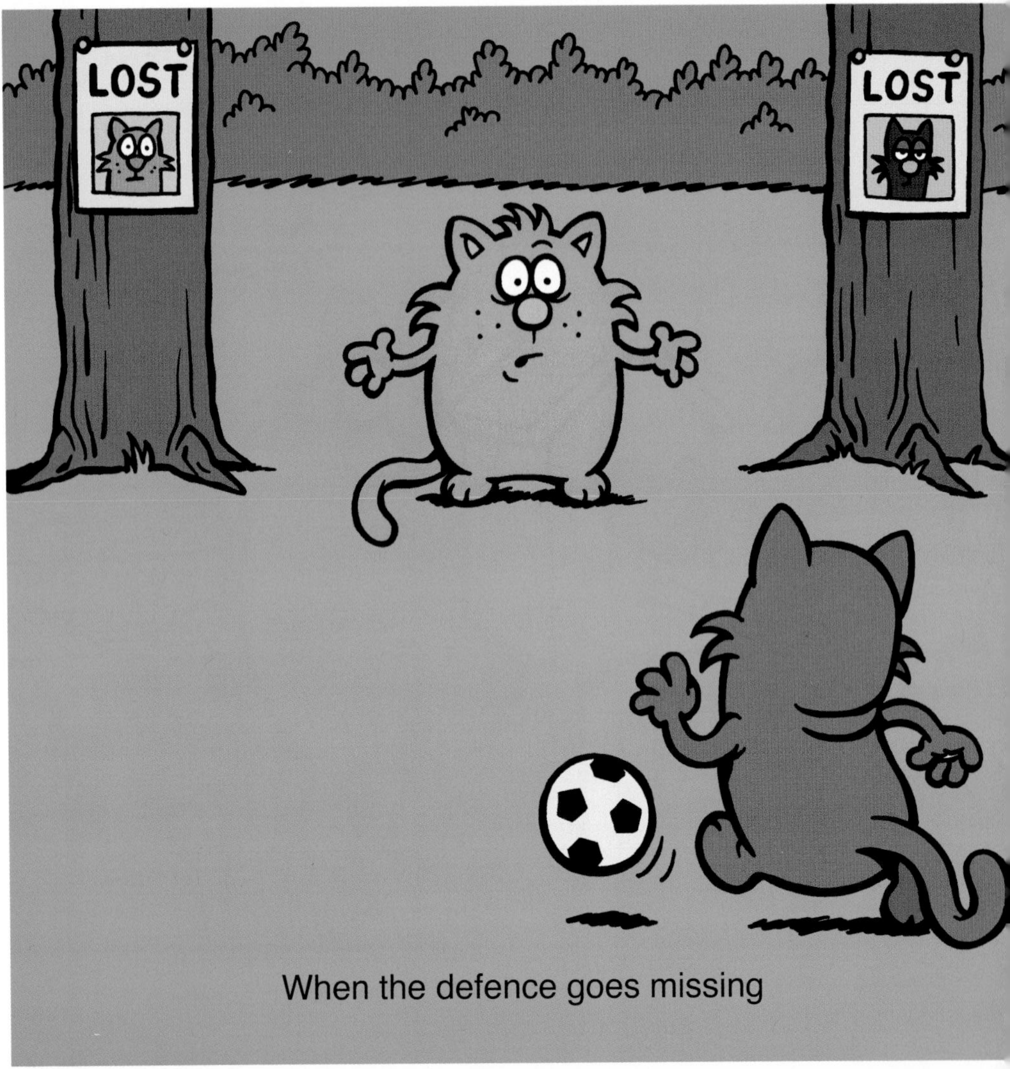
LOST
LOST

When the defence goes missing

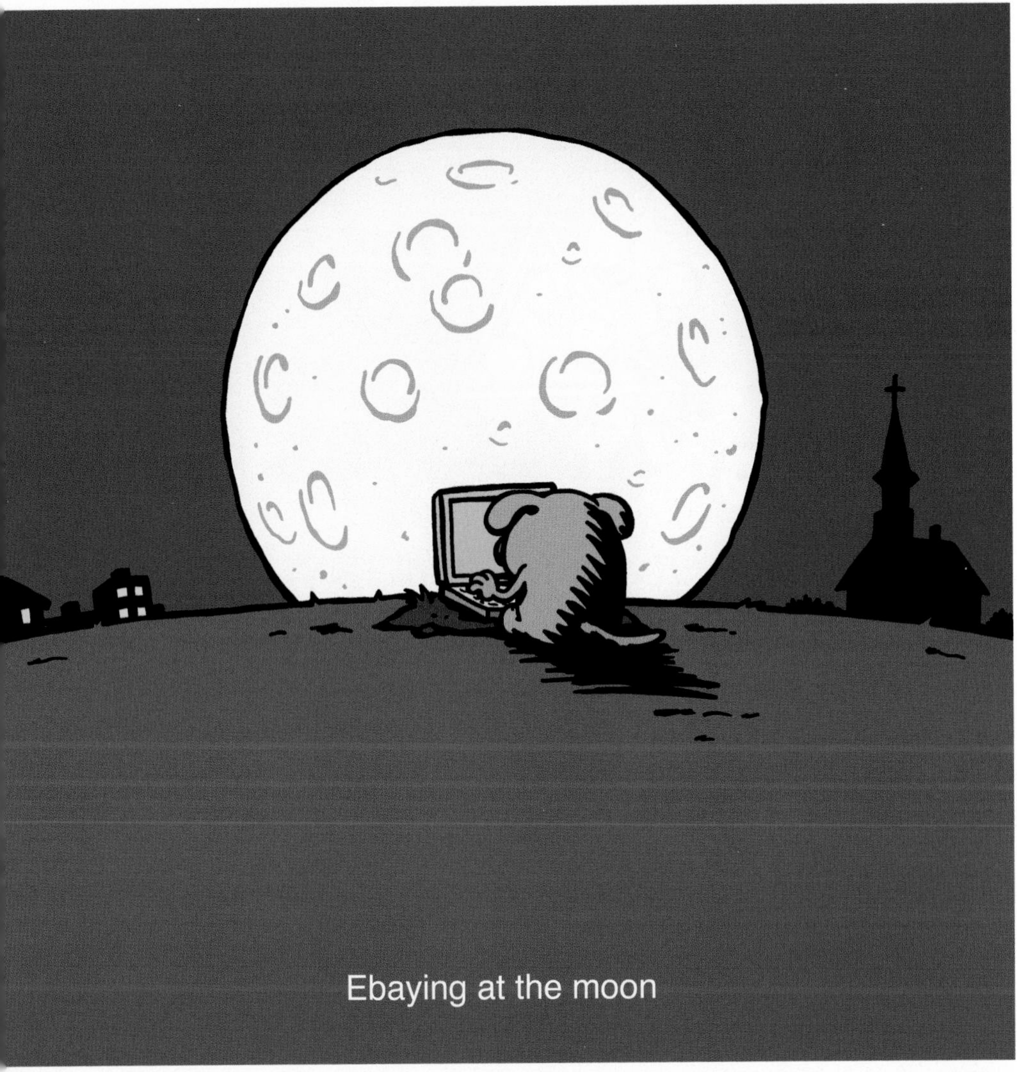

Ebaying at the moon

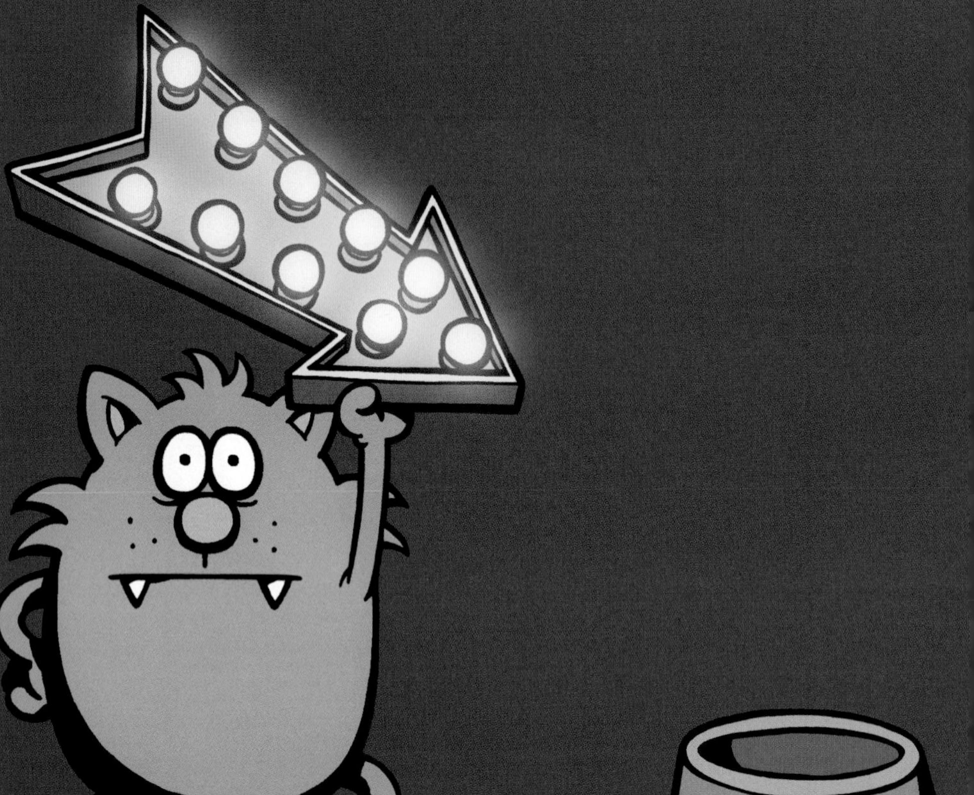

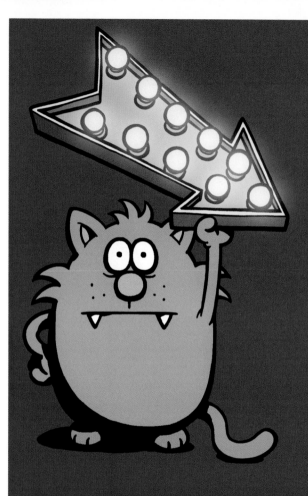

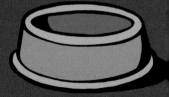

When cats hint

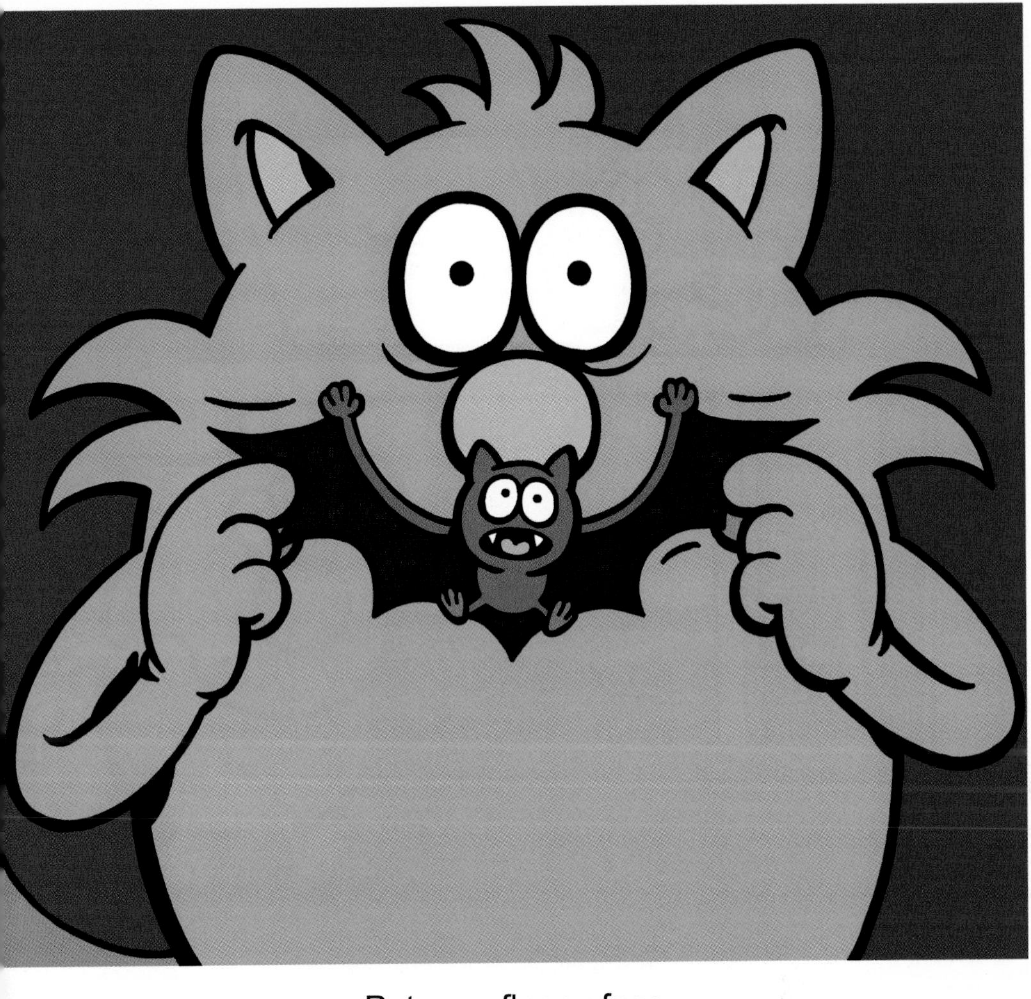

Put on a flappy face

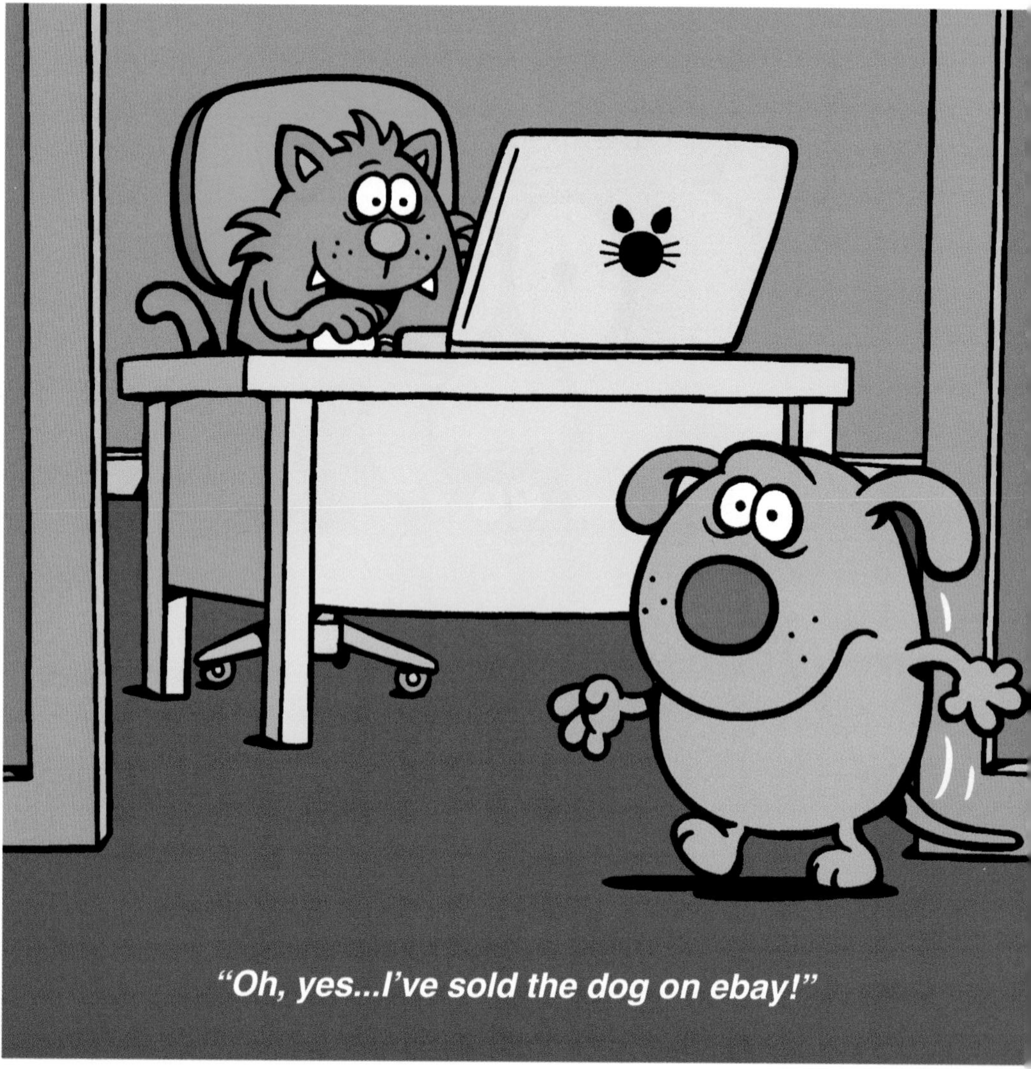

"Oh, yes...I've sold the dog on ebay!"

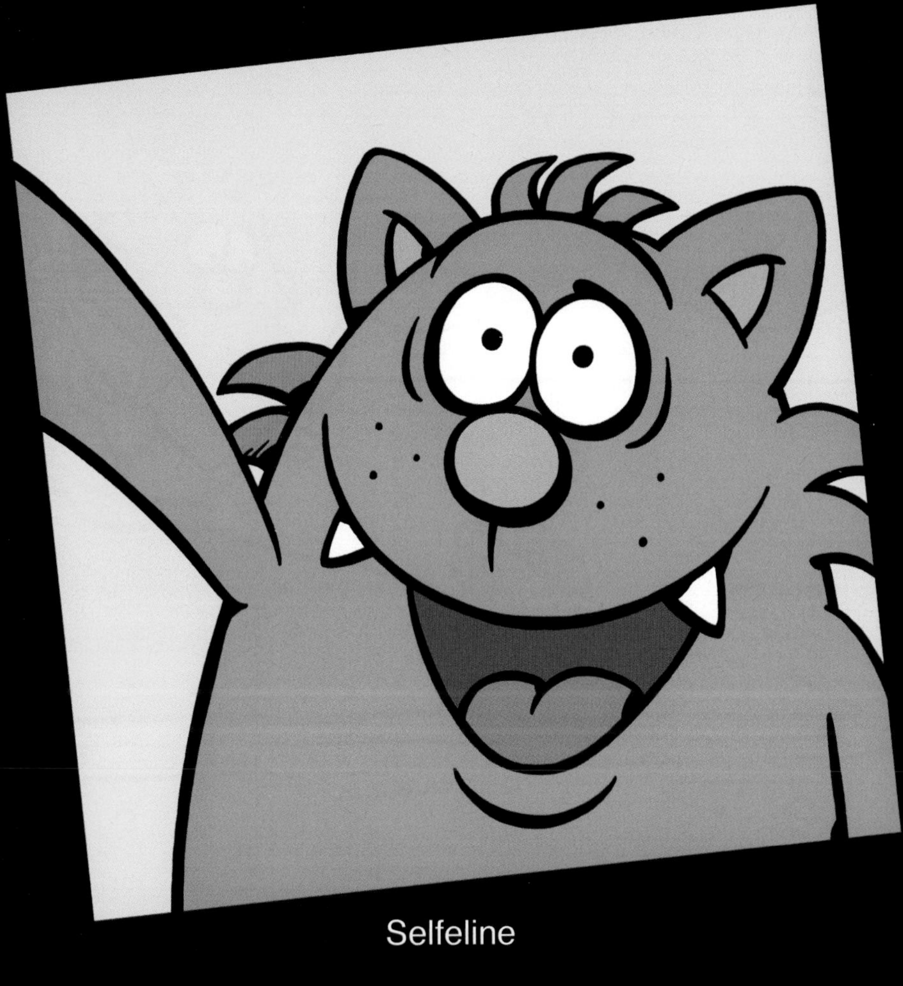

Selfeline

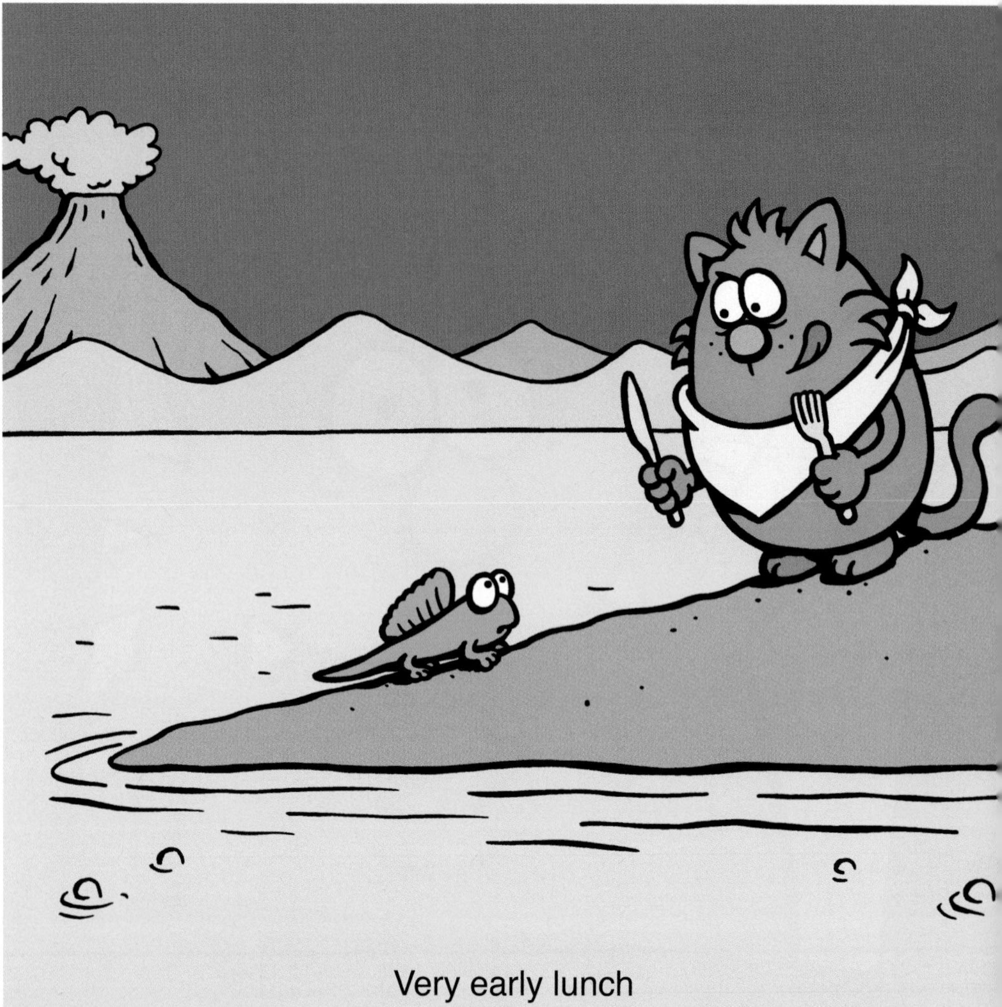

Very early lunch

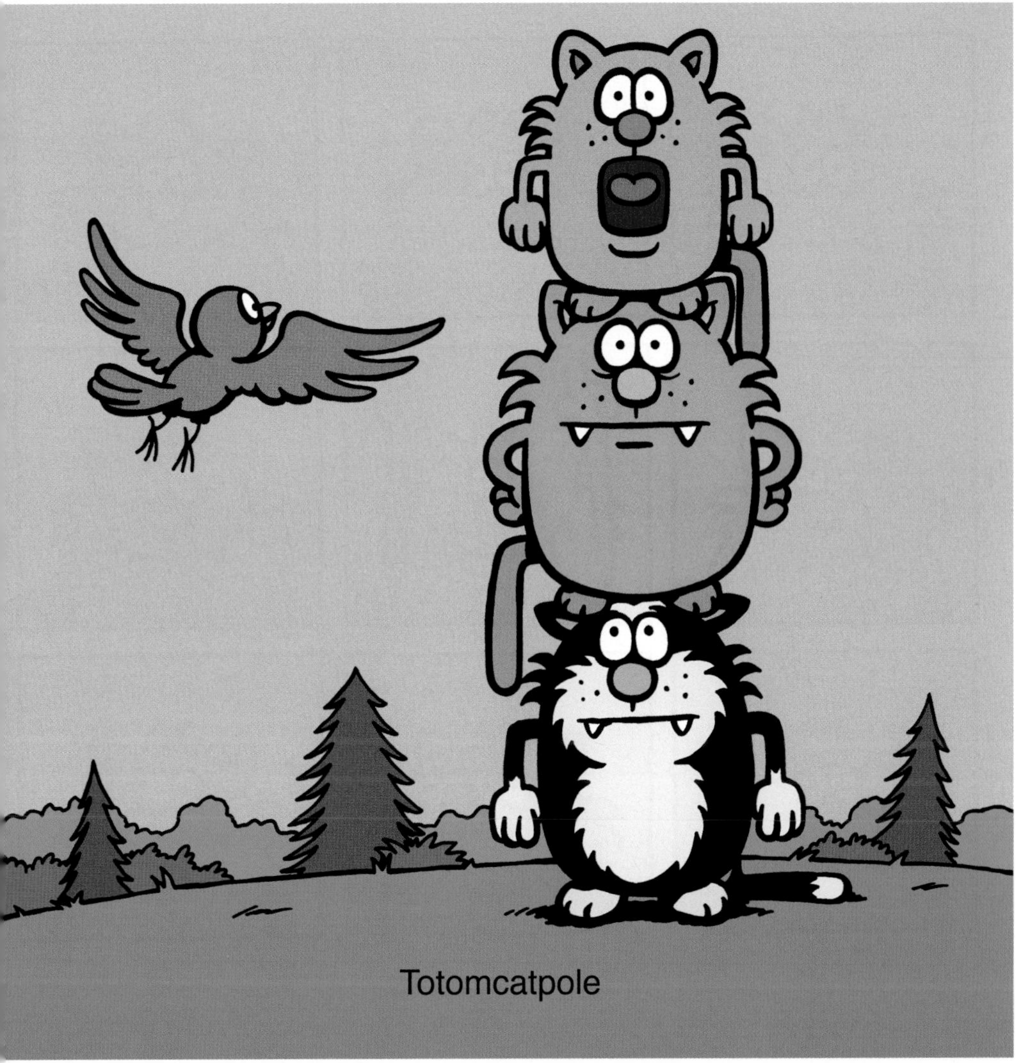

Totomcatpole

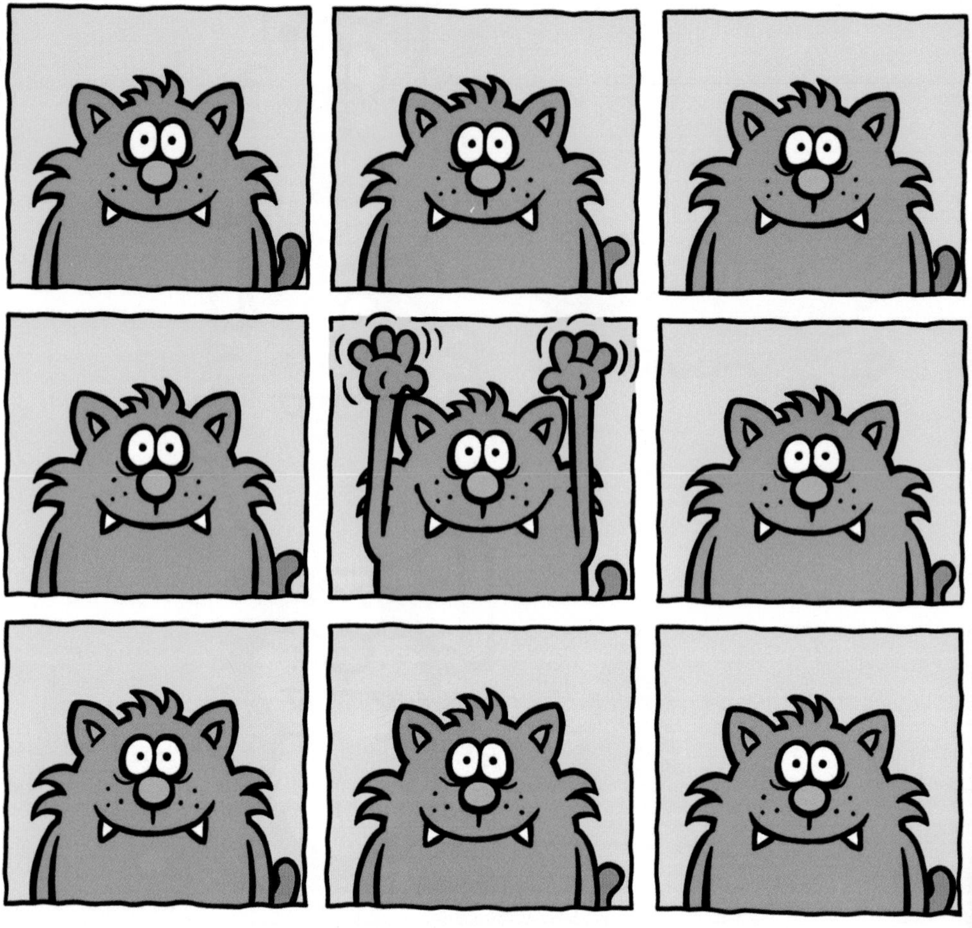

Dramatic paws

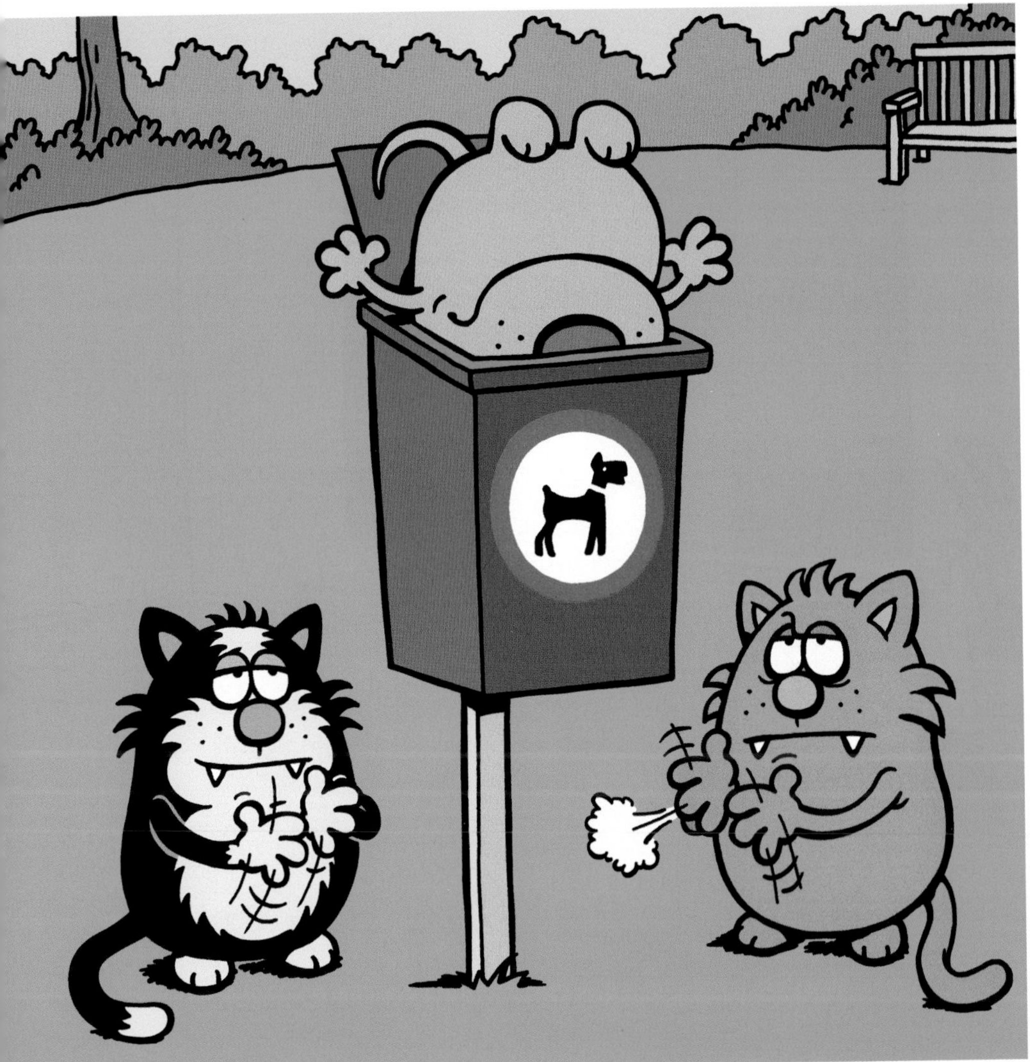

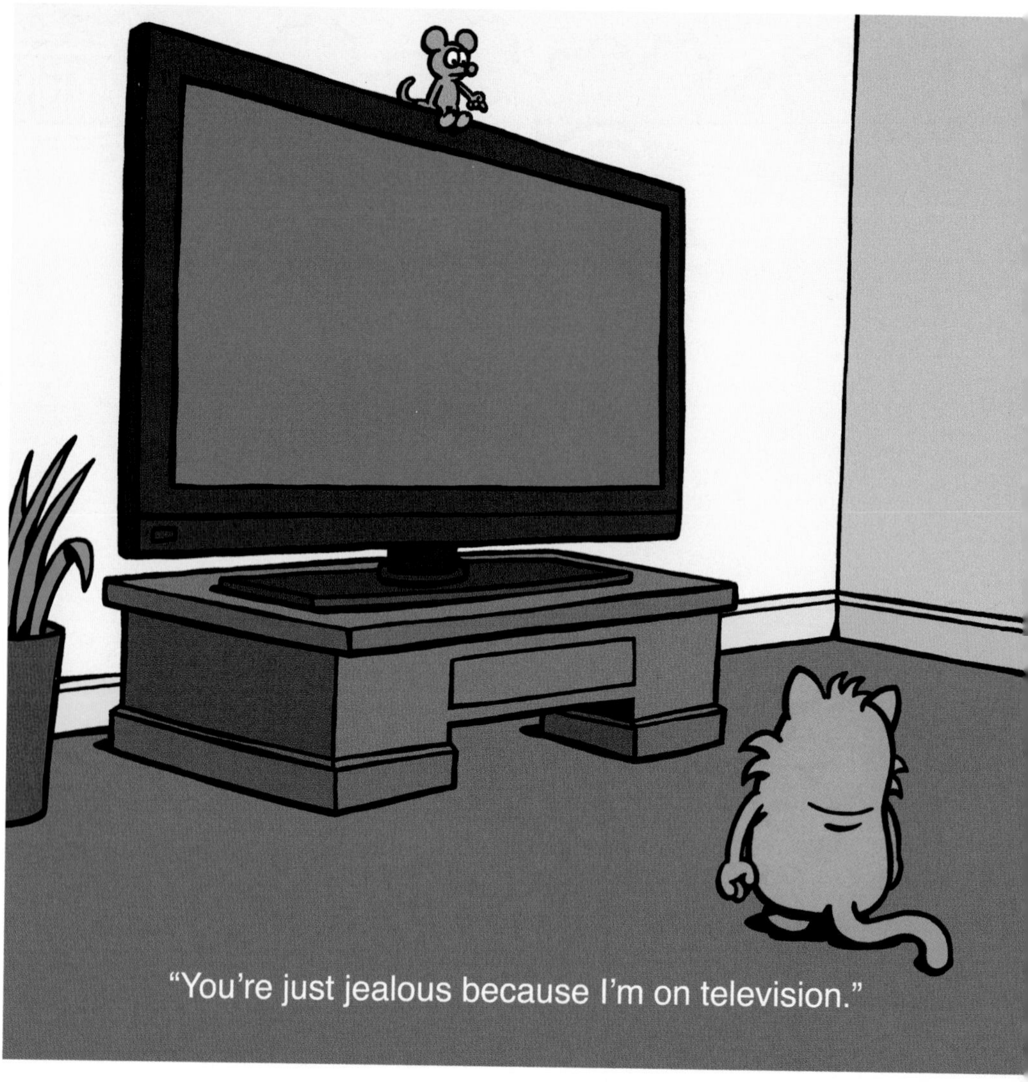

“You’re just jealous because I’m on television.”

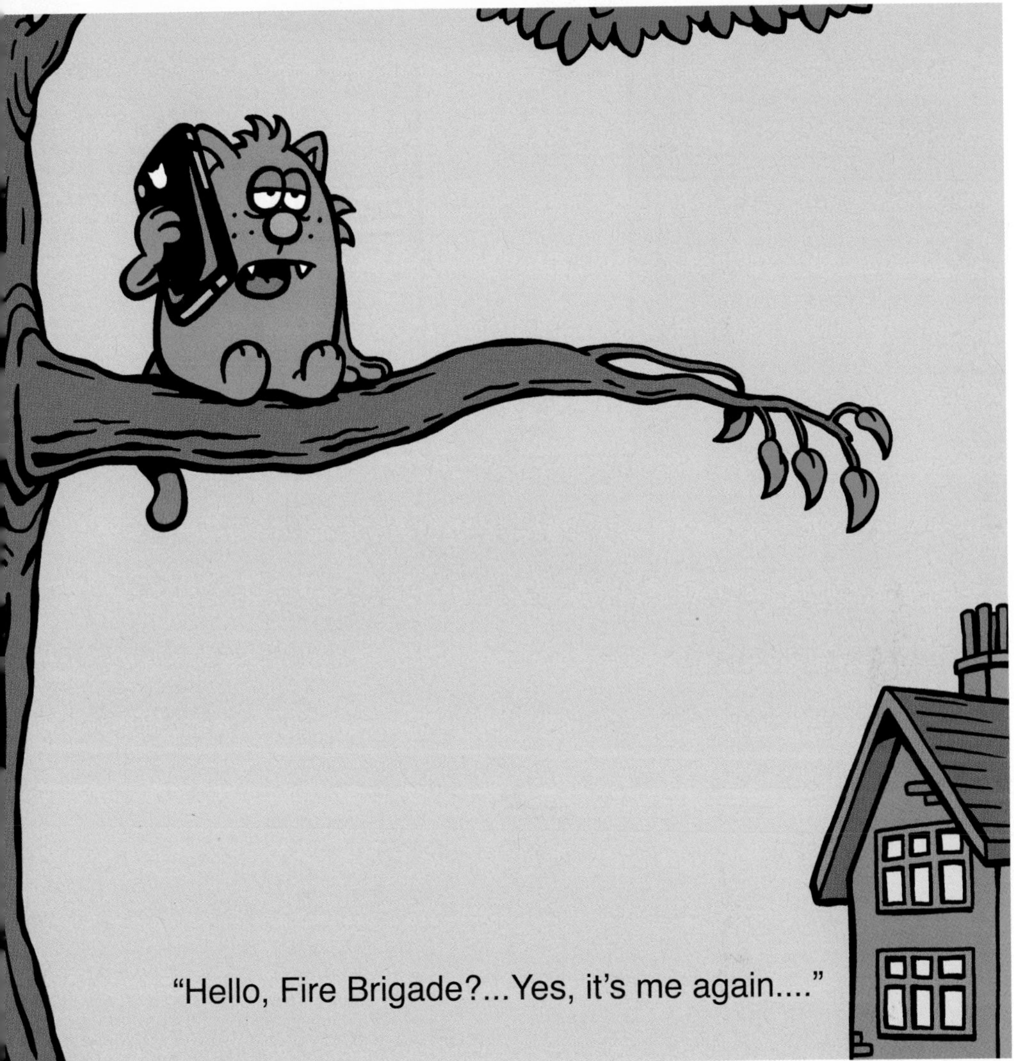

“Hello, Fire Brigade?...Yes, it’s me again....”

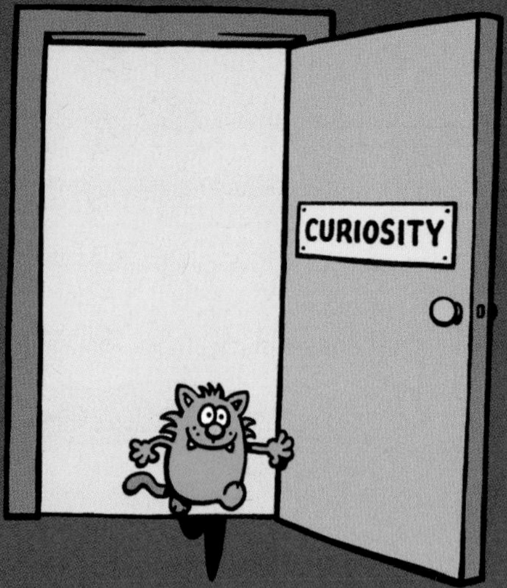
CURIOSITY